METHODS FOR LUKE

In *Methods for Luke*, four leading scholars demonstrate how different interpretive methods provide insight into the Gospel of Luke. Introducing contemporary perspectives on historical criticism, feminist criticism, narrative criticism, and Latino interpretation, they illustrate these approaches to New Testament study by examining either the parable of the rich man and Lazarus (Luke 16:19–31) or Jesus' warning regarding the scribes and the story of the women with two small coins (Luke 20:45–21:4). The use of two "set texts" enables readers to understand how method makes a difference in the reading of the same text.

Joel B. Green is Professor of New Testament Interpretation and Associate Dean for the Center for Advanced Theological Studies, Fuller Theological Seminary. He is the author, co-author, or editor of twenty-eight books, including *The Theology of the Gospel of Luke* (1995) and, most recently, *Body, Soul, and Human Life: The Nature of Humanity in the Bible* (2008). He has published numerous essays in a variety of symposia and journals, including *Zeitschrift für die neutestamentliche Wissenschaft, Journal for the Study of the New Testament,* and *Catholic Biblical Quarterly.*

METHODS IN BIBLICAL INTERPRETATION

The Methods in Biblical Interpretation (MBI) series introduces students and general readers to both older and emerging methodologies for understanding the Hebrew Scriptures and the New Testament. Newer methods brought about by the globalization of biblical studies and by concerns with the "world in front of the text" – like new historicism, feminist criticism, postcolonial/liberationist criticism, and rhetorical criticism – are well represented in the series. Classical methods that fall under the more traditional historical–critical banner – such as source criticism, form criticism, and redaction criticism – are also covered, though always with an understanding of how their interactions with emerging methodologies and new archaeological discoveries have affected their interpretive uses.

An MBI volume contains separate chapters from different well-known scholars. Each scholar first elucidates the history and purposes of an interpretive method, then outlines the promise of the method in the context of a single biblical book, and finally shows the method "in action" by applying it to a specific biblical passage. The results serve as a primer for understanding different methods within the shared space of common texts, enabling real, comparative analysis for students, clergy, and anyone interested in a deeper and broader understanding of the Bible. A glossary of key terms, the translation of all ancient languages, and an annotated bibliography – arranged by method – help new, serious readers navigate the difficult but rewarding field of biblical interpretation.

Volumes in the series

Methods for Exodus, edited by Thomas B. Dozeman
Methods for the Psalms, edited by Esther Marie Menn
Methods for Matthew, edited by Mark Allan Powell
Methods for Luke, edited by Joel B. Green

Methods for Luke

Edited by

JOEL B. GREEN
Fuller Theological Seminary

CAMBRIDGE
UNIVERSITY PRESS

CAMBRIDGE UNIVERSITY PRESS
Cambridge, New York, Melbourne, Madrid, Cape Town, Singapore,
São Paulo, Delhi, Dubai, Tokyo

Cambridge University Press
32 Avenue of the Americas, New York, NY 10013-2473, USA

www.cambridge.org
Information on this title: www.cambridge.org/9780521717816

First published 2010

Printed in the United States of America

A catalog record for this publication is available from the British Library.

Library of Congress Cataloging in Publication data

Methods for Luke / edited by Joel B. Green.
p.   cm. – (Methods in biblical interpretation)
Includes bibliographical references and index.
ISBN 978-0-521-88912-4 (hardback) – ISBN 978-0-521-71781-6 (pbk.)
1. Bible. N.T. Luke – Hermeneutics.   2. Bible. N.T. Luke – Criticism, interpretation, etc.
I. Green, Joel B., 1956–
BS2595.52.M47   2010
226.4'0601 – dc22   2009036860

ISBN 978-0-521-88912-4 Hardback
ISBN 978-0-521-71781-6 Paperback

Contents

Contributors

Justo L. González, a native of Cuba, received his Ph.D. in historical theology from Yale University in 1961. Since then he has taught in several institutions, both in the United States and overseas, and has published more than a hundred books, mostly on historical theology and biblical interpretation. Among the best known are *The Story of Christianity* (2 vols.) and *A History of Christian Thought* (3 vols.). Besides his earned degrees, he holds four honorary doctorates. His main current interest is developing support for Hispanic theological education.

Joel B. Green is Professor of New Testament Interpretation and Associate Dean for the Center for Advanced Theological Studies, Fuller Theological Seminary. He is the author, co-author, or editor of twenty-eight books, including *The Theology of the Gospel of Luke* (1995) and, most recently, *Body, Soul, and Human Life: The Nature of Humanity in the Bible* (2008). He was New Testament editor for *The New Interpreter's Dictionary of the Bible* (5 vols.) and is general editor for the forthcoming revision of *Dictionary of Jesus and the Gospels*.

Clare K. Rothschild, Assistant Professor in the Department of Theology at Lewis University, is the author of *Baptist Traditions and Q* (2005) and *Luke-Acts and the Rhetoric of History* (2004). She is currently working on her third book, *Hebrews as Pseudograph: The History and Significance of the Pauline Attribution of Hebrews*. Professor Rothschild has held teaching positions at McCormick Seminary, Xavier

University, Saint Mary's College (Notre Dame), and DePaul University and was recently appointed to serve as editor of *Early Christianity*, a new journal to be published by Mohr Siebeck.

Turid Karlsen Seim, Professor of New Testament and Early Christian Literature at the University of Oslo since 1991 and Director of The Norwegian Institute in Rome since 2007, is the author of *The Double Message: Patterns of Gender in Luke-Acts* (1994). She conducted an international project on "Metamorphoses: Resurrection, Body and Transformative Practices in Early Christianity" in 2008 and is the author of multiple articles on Luke-Acts. Professor Seim is presently working on the Gospel of John, as well as pursuing her former studies on Luke-Acts.

↓

Reading Luke

Joel B. Green

Contemporary study of the Gospel of Luke takes its starting point from the mid-twentieth-century publication of Hans Conzelmann's redaction-critical study, *The Theology of St Luke*.[1] In Conzelmann's hands, the distinctive voice of Luke the evangelist emerged, leaving in its wake earlier judgments of Luke as the voice of Paul (who sometimes misunderstood the Pauline message) or as one so slavishly devoted to his sources that he was incapable of any theological contribution of his own. Arguably, the pillars of Conzelmann's perspective on Luke – for example, his emphasis on the delay of the Parousia, his apology for Rome, or his presentation of Jesus' ministry as a Satan-free period – have been felled, one by one, by subsequent scholarship. Nevertheless, Conzelmann's work altered the course of historical study of the Third Gospel, paved the way for what would become first composition – and then literary-critical analysis of Luke – and set the interpretive agenda

---

[1] Hans Conzelmann, *The Theology of St Luke* (London: Faber & Faber, 1960).
   For general introductions to the Gospel of Luke, see Mark Allan Powell, *What Are They Saying about Luke?* (New York: Paulist, 1989); and, more recently, F. Scott Spencer, *The Gospel of Luke and Acts of the Apostles* (IBT; Nashville, Tenn.: Abingdon, 2008).
   For an abbreviated survey of contemporary study of the interpretation of Luke, see Anthony C. Thiselton, "The Hermeneutical Dynamics of 'Reading Luke' as Interpretation, Reflection and Formation," in *Reading Luke: Interpretation, Reflection, Formation* (ed. Craig G. Bartholomew, Joel B. Green, and Anthony C. Thiselton; SAHS 6; Grand Rapids, Mich.: Zondervan, 1985), 3–52. For a more exhaustive account, see François Bovon, *Luke the Theologian: Fifty-five Years of Research (1950–2005)* (2nd rev. ed.; Waco, Tex.: Baylor University Press, 2006).

in ways that would open the door to a wide array of other, especially
social-scientific and political, approaches to reading Luke.

If, in retrospect, Conzelmann was the catalyst for these new path-
ways in interpreting Luke, it is also true that he shared this role with
many others in biblical studies more generally. Similar work on the
other Synoptic Gospels dates to the same period, for example, with
Günther Bornkamm and his students' work on the Gospel of Matthew
and Willi Marxen's work on Mark.[2] Alongside the rise of redaction
criticism, though, new winds were blowing – some from philosophical hermeneutics, such as the work of Hans-Georg Gadamer, with
its emphasis on understanding as the fusion of the horizons of the
text with the horizons of the reader; and some from university-based
literary theorists, whose navigation of the triad, author – text – reader,
led to a proliferation of interpretive interests and reading protocols.[3]
We may add to this three simple, but extraordinarily important, realities: (1) higher education – and with it both seminary education and
graduate education in religion – has become increasingly accessible
to people of myriad backgrounds, measured, for example, in terms of
race and ethnicity, sex, and socioeconomics; (2) the church that spon-
sors and profits from major sectors of biblical studies has become
increasingly ethnic in the United States and, globally, increasingly
indigenous to the southern and eastern hemispheres; and (3) due to
the geographical shifts in the church's populations and heightened
ecumenical interests, the analogical style of biblical interpretation
at home in Eastern Orthodoxy has begun to be heard in a western
church and guild for which such interpretive protocols remain quite
alien. Such broader realities as these have raised in recent decades and
continue to raise serious questions for traditional biblical studies. The
questions include concerns with the assumptions in which traditional
biblical scholarship has been grounded, the methods it has accredited,

---

[2] Willi Marxsen, *Mark the Evangelist* (Nashville, Tenn.: Abingdon, 1969); Günther
   Bornkamm, Gerhard Barth, and Heinz Joachim Held, *Tradition and Interpretation
   in Matthew* (London: SCM, 1963).
[3] See Hans-Georg Gadamer, *Truth and Method* (2nd rev. ed.; New York: Crossroad,
   1990); Stephen Greenblatt and Giles Gunn, eds., *Redrawing the Boundaries: The
   Transformation of English and American Literary Studies* (New York: The Modern
   Language Association of America, 1992).

and the curricula by which it has perpetuated itself. These sorts of considerations and currents often parade under the cultural heading of postmodernism.

By its very nature, postmodernism defies classification and definition, but surely one of the characteristics of our postmodern age is our awareness that acts of interpretation are by their very nature efforts to constrain meaning. Critical study, whatever shape it might take, shares an interest in articulating and deploying canons for adjudicating among various and competing readings of the same text. Why do we prefer this reading over that one? What reasons can we muster to support this interpretation or exclude that one? Another prominent feature of our current cultural situation would be not only the presence of multiple interests but our recognition of the multiple interests that shape our interpretive agenda and influence the interpretive boundaries we draw and/or are willing to allow.

In important and perhaps unanticipated ways, these myriad interests seem to comport well with some key ingredients of the biblical materials and our study of them. Let me give examples.

(1) How we got our Bible is a lengthy, dusty process, significant points of which are empirically lost to us. We can imagine the movement from various historical events to the crafting of word-accounts to the formation of written accounts gathered and redacted into the "final form" of the Bible sitting on our desks and bed stands. We can discern within the text itself seams and features of orality suggestive of these procedural actions and their settings. The point, of course, is that both the final form of the text and each step in its formation invite study, with different methods more appropriate to one formative stage than another.

(2) The Bible is an aggregate of multiple genres – for example, historical narrative, poetry, letters, prophetic oracle, and apocalypse. Because each genre is "a specific way of visualizing a given part of reality,"[4] it represents specific social interaction and a particularized vision of reality, and resists easy integration into a reader's (or a

---

[4] Mikhail Bakhtin, "Theory of Genres," in *Mikhail Bakhtin: Creation of a Prosaics* (ed. Gary Saul Morson and Caryl Emerson; Stanford, Calif.: Stanford University Press, 1990), 271–305 (275).

readerly community's) theoretical system. The pluralism of the Bible's literary forms, then, invites a corresponding pluralism of interpretive protocols.

(3) The Bible has been and is today read in multiple settings, in relation to more-or-less circumscribed "publics." Reading the Bible within the church invites gestures and protocols that in some societies are not acceptable in a university or other nonreligiously oriented education setting. A statement published jointly by The Bible Literacy Project, Inc., and the First Amendment Center and endorsed by such organizations as People for the American Way Foundation, the Baptist Joint Committee on Public Affairs, and the Society of Biblical Literature documents the widely shared view that study about the Bible can be an important part of a comprehensive education in literature and history courses. "Knowledge of biblical stories and concepts contributes to our understanding of literature, history, law, art, and contemporary society."[5] Public schools, then, might develop curriculum relative to the Bible and literature, the Bible and history, or the Bible and world religions. These contexts for reading the Bible might support a variety of methodological approaches, and some of these might also be at home in an ecclesial context. But an ecclesial context for engaging the Bible would likely encourage additional sensibilities and interpretive procedures judged unsavory and even ruled out of court by The Bible Literacy Project and the First Amendment Center. These might include, for example, a commitment to the theological coherence of the canon of Scripture, a commitment to the Rule of Faith as a lens through which to read the message of Scripture, or a vision of the work of interpretation as self-involving, as a willingness to be taken in by the text.[6]

[5] "The Bible and Public Schools: A First Amendment Guide" (Nashville, Tenn.: First Amendment Center, 1999), p. 5. The Society of Biblical Literature Council added its name to the list of organizations endorsing the statement on April 29, 2006.
[6] See, for example, Richard B. Hays, "Reading the Bible with Eyes of Faith: The Practice of Theological Exegesis," *Journal of Theological Interpretation* 1 (2007): 5–21; Matthew Levering, *Participatory Biblical Exegesis: A Theology of Biblical Interpretation* (Notre Dame, Ind.: University of Notre Dame Press, 2008); Joel B. Green, *Seized by Truth: Reading the Bible as Scripture* (Nashville, Tenn.: Abingdon, 2007).

(4) This last point regarding the multiple settings of biblical interpretation deserves expansion in another direction, one that takes seriously not only the major contextual categories of church and university. Because we find more and more diversity among the peoples engaging in disciplined study of the Bible we should not be surprised by the corresponding diversity in the interpretive interests and needs people bring with them to the Bible – and, then, the concomitant diversity of approaches by which the biblical materials are accessed. If African-American interpretation today focuses on such concerns as responding to racist interpretations of biblical texts, recovering and analyzing the African presence in the Bible, and intercultural interpretation of biblical texts from the perspective of African-American readers, for example, we need not look far to understand why this is so. They grow out of the complex history of African Americans and the Bible over the last two or three centuries. What motivates us to engage with biblical texts, what we go searching for, and what we find are determined at least in part by where we stand. And where we stand entails any number of features – some theological, some sociological, some philosophical, some geographical, and so on.

Why should we be interested in *method*? Our interests arise precisely because of the nature of the biblical materials and the varying interests and needs of the Bible's readers. If our situation has the potential for generating a cacophony of readings, then *method* surfaces as a way of bringing some discipline to our interpretive work. By "discipline" I do not mean to refer to *technique*, as though interpretation could be reduced to an objective, paint-by-the-numbers or step-by-step procedure, a machine into which texts might be poured and out of which "meaning" might be drawn. A method might be known by the steps comprising its rules of engagement, but method can also refer more to the sensibilities and commitments by which we engage texts. Here, then, I am more concerned with discipline in terms of the transparency with which one practices a particular form of biblical interpretation: What assumptions about meaning are central? What are the aims of this pathway to interpretation? What protocols are followed? In other words, as with research methodology more generally, by discipline I am referring both to one's willingness and ability to show how this reading was achieved, and to the openness of interpreters to have their approach to interpretation and the results of their reading queried in relation to their coherence with the text being read.

From this perspective, none of us who engage in disciplined reading of the Bible can regard ourselves as neutral observers of a textual object. We have our reasons and our cultural histories, and this disqualifies whatever claims we might have wanted to make about our practices of dispassionate exegesis or our indifference to the outcomes of our interpretive work. If neutrality is not an option, however, the same could not be said of objectivity, which can and must be the hallmark of disciplined study of the Bible. Following the useful distinction made by Thomas Haskell, I am capable of objectivity even though I have no ledge on which to stand and from which to operate as a neutral interpreter. By "neutrality," then, I refer to preconceptions, hunches, biases, and aims that guide my interpretive work. By "objectivity," I refer, with Haskell, to the capacity for self-overcoming, for considering readings and arguments counter to our own, for honesty and fairness in our representation of the views of others – that is, to those habits and practices that make public discourse possible.[7]

New Testament (NT) studies today offers a veritable smorgasbord of interpretive methods, four of which are on display in the chapters that follow. The astute reader will recognize that, although only four approaches are sketched and illustrated, in their own ways these four are representative of major currents in the field. Clare Rothschild's chapter on historical criticism, for example, articulates much of what we now regard as traditional biblical studies, occupied as it has been for the last two centuries with the prehistory of the text: the history of the text's formation, the history presumed by the text, and the history to which the text in its redacted form bears witness. At the same time, however, Rothschild demonstrates how historical criticism has begun

---

[7] Thomas L. Haskell, "Objectivity Is Not Neutrality: Rhetoric versus Practice in Peter Novick's *That Noble Dream*," in *Objectivity Is Not Neutrality: Explanatory Schemes in History* (Baltimore, Md.: The Johns Hopkins University Press, 1998), 145–73.

to account more fully for less traditional concerns such as literary art and persuasion. Her chapter thus demonstrates what is also true of the other three – first, that these methods continue to evolve and, second, that the direction of their development is influenced by considerations often associated with other methodological commitments.

Turid Seim's chapter sketches the state of the art in feminist criticism of the NT, demonstrating especially how the term "feminist criticism" actually refers not to one methodological approach but to a plethora of criticisms. In this case, "feminist" refers to a set of commitments and sensibilities that pervade other interpretive interests, be they historical, textual, readerly, or more broadly hermeneutical. With Seim's chapter we have a parade example of the distinction I have drawn between neutrality and objectivity in NT study. On the one hand, one of the most powerful and enduring lessons of feminist criticism has been its rejection of the idea of an uninterested, presuppositionless reading of Scripture. On the other, feminist criticism of Luke's Gospel, as Seim articulates it, explores the role of women in the Lukan narrative without distorting the textual evidence in one direction or by participating in wishful thinking.

In his chapter on narrative criticism, Green attempts to break narrative study out of the side room in which it is often placed, as though it were interested merely in the Gospels and Acts as self-contained reservoirs of literary artistry. Instead, he argues, narrative criticism of these NT texts cannot escape these texts' historical dimensions and must account for those whose reading helps to construct how and what these narratives mean. Today, narrative critics are developing the discipline so as to account for how narratives are implicated in cultural criticism as well as how they engage, and are engaged by, their manifold readers. In this way, narrative study increasingly blurs the lines between author, text, and reader.

Finally, Justo González provides a Latino perspective on reading Luke. He articulates from a Latino perspective the wrongheadedness of an enterprise focused on method *per se*, then shows how biography – including both autobiography and the story of one's interpretive community – shapes interpretive interests. González does not attempt to speak for Latina readers of Scripture, no more than he tries to speak for the entire Hispanic world. Nevertheless, for those willing to follow him, he navigates a hermeneutical path for which we have multiple parallels in other interpretive communities (African-American, African, Asian-American, etc.) seeking to take seriously how their stories shape, or might shape, their practices of reading. Throughout these chapters, we learn that what we see in these texts depends a lot on where we are standing, and what we are looking for.

Each of the chapters that follow has two major sections. The first is a presentation of a particular method and its relevance for the Gospel of Luke. The second provides a hands-on analysis of one of two set texts – either Luke 16:19–31 (the Parable of the Rich Man and Lazarus) or Luke 20:45–21:4 (Jesus' Warning about the Scribes and the story of the Woman and Two Small Coins) – in which the author places that method on display.

2

↓

Historical Criticism

Clare K. Rothschild

The historical–critical method encompasses a variety of strategies for eliciting meaning from a premodern literary text. The most prominent of these subspecies are text, source, form, redaction, rhetorical, and social-scientific criticism.[1] Although distinctive, each approach prioritizes comparative analysis of a text in its literary and historical contexts – involving cultural, social, political, religious, and other aspects. An investigation of early Christian texts from a historical–critical perspective implies close examination of a passage using any or all of the pertinent critical techniques listed previously.

In this chapter I sketch the emergence of the historical–critical method in the field of biblical studies and describe its suitability for understanding the Gospel of Luke. Following this background, I analyze Luke 20:45–21:4 by means of this method, showing how manipulation of traditional source material, in this case the author's version of Mark, best explains the author's narrative strategy, which in turn helps to reveal the author's first goal: to write the first credible history of early Christianity.

[1] Edgar Krentz, *The Historical-Critical Method* (Eugene, Ore.: Wipf and Stock, 2002 [1975]). Cf. also Van A. Harvey, *The Historian and the Believer* (New York: Macmillan, 1966).

A BRIEF HISTORY OF THE HISTORICAL–CRITICAL METHOD

"Higher criticism" was the name given to study of the Bible as any other ancient text, that is, as composed by human beings during particular phases in history.[2] In contrast, "lower criticism" was the attempt to understand biblical texts on the basis of internal evidence alone. The Dutch scholar Erasmus (1466–1536) might be credited as the first to study the Bible critically, although many of his methods are identifiable in the work of earlier scholars and theologians. "Higher criticism" developed in Europe from the mid-eighteenth century to the early twentieth century. Representatives include Jean Astruc (1684–1766), Johann Salomo Semler (1725–91), Johann Gottfried Eichhorn (1752–1827), Ferdinand Christian Baur (1792–1860), and Julius Wellhausen (1844–1918). Today higher and lower criticisms together constitute what is commonly referred to as the historical–critical method. Lower criticism is now designated text criticism, and higher criticism takes the form of source, form, redaction, rhetorical, and social-scientific criticism. A brief summary of each approach clarifies its usefulness for understanding the New Testament (NT).

Text Criticism

Textual criticism seeks to establish the Greek text in the absence of autographs. None of the surviving Greek manuscripts of the NT was handwritten by its author. Rather, all of the earliest surviving NT manuscripts are copies.[3] As one would expect, the copying process

---

[2] In this section I rely on the following introductory textbooks: Dennis C. Duling and Norman Perrin, *Proclamation and Parenesis, Myth and History* (3rd ed.; New York: Harcourt Brace, 1974), esp. 5–26; Bart D. Ehrman, *The New Testament: A Historical Introduction to the Early Christian Writings* (4th ed.; New York: Oxford University Press, 2007); Krentz, *Historical-Critical Method*; Werner Georg Kümmel, *The New Testament: The History of the Investigation of Its Problems* (Nashville, Tenn.: Abingdon, 1972); Mark Allan Powell, *Fortress Introduction to the Gospels* (Minneapolis, Minn.: Fortress, 1998); Udo Schnelle, *The History and Theology of the New Testament Writings* (Minneapolis, Minn.: Fortress, 1998).

[3] See Bruce M. Metzger, *The Text of the New Testament: Its Transmission, Corruption, and Restoration* (3rd ed.; New York: Oxford University Press, 1992).

incurred numerous errors. Although most are minor, some errors, or "variants," intentionally altered the meaning of the texts. Scribes or copyists deliberately added or subtracted from a text, for example, to conform a passage to later Christian doctrine or to defend a scribe or other group against opponents. Careful evaluation of these NT manuscript variants is known as textual criticism. Textual criticism assesses variants as a means of reconstructing hypothetical versions of now-lost original documents.

Although it was once considered the most scientific of historical–critical methods, today textual criticism faces a dilemma. According to a highly respected practitioner of the method, Eldon J. Epp, textual criticism is currently undergoing a "loss of innocence," coming to grips with the limits of the method.[4] The crisis stems partly from recognition that the quest for the original texts is futile. However, the crisis also stems from recognition of the value of the work of other types of NT interpreters. Although exegetes were once reliant on textual critics for reconstructions of the Greek text, today careful, well-trained exegetes are equally important to this process of reconstruction. Epp writes: "A point to be noted is that not only does textual criticism affect exegesis, but exegesis affects textual criticism in case after case."[5] Using Adela Yarbro Collins's careful analysis of Mark 1:1 as exemplar, Epp concludes,

This summary of one exegete's careful examination of a range of considerations that enter into a "text-critical" decision shows that drawing a conclusion about which text to interpret is much broader than a mechanical application of certain "criteria" or "principles" of textual criticism. Rather, the immediate and larger context of the writing itself and of the historical-theological setting from which it arose and in which it later functioned may all be relevant factors in deciding between/among variant readings. Very often these cases are difficult, and all too frequently judgments must be made in the absence of full confidence.[6]

---

[4] Eldon J. Epp, *Junia: The First Woman Apostle* (Minneapolis, Minn.: Fortress, 2005), 12–13.
[5] Epp, *Junia*, 7–8.
[6] Epp, *Junia*, 9.

In contrast to other classification systems, the system for classifying NT manuscripts was not developed in a single sitting. Rather, it
developed gradually, resulting in a system that is sometimes cumber-
some and difficult for students to understand. For example, manuscripts are grouped according to a few different criteria. Papyri are
manuscripts made from the papyrus plant growing in abundance on
the banks of the Nile River.[7] Whereas in damper climates manuscripts
tend to disintegrate over time, the hot and dry climate of Egypt helped
to preserve these manuscripts. Papyri are among our earliest surviving
manuscripts of the NT. Today ninety-six NT papyri are cited in official lists. Almost all of these papyri were, at one time, parts of codices
or books. Papyrologists label papyri with a letter "P" plus a number.
Dating to *circa* 125 C.E., the earliest papyrus of the NT is P[52] – a very
small fragment of the Gospel of John (front side, John 18:31–33; back
side, John 18:37–39).

Other manuscripts are not classified by the material on which they
were written, but by the kind of script they use, either uncials (block
capital letters) or minuscules (cursive script). Although block capital letters were also used on papyrus, the expression "uncials" refers
to manuscripts with uncial characters on vellum (or parchment) or
paper. Vellum is animal hide that has been processed for writing.
Although it is commonly thought that the papyri represent our oldest
witnesses of the NT, of the approximately 300 surviving uncials, some
are almost as old as the papyri. Most of the uncials have nicknames
indicating where they were found or who found them. The most
famous uncial manuscript is called Codex Sinaiticus. It was discovered by Constantin von Tischendorf on his third visit to the Monastery
of St. Catherine at the foot of Mount Sinai in Egypt in 1859. The tale
about its finding may be legendary, but it is nevertheless insightful
about the serendipitous nature of many manuscript discoveries:

On the afternoon of this day I was taking a walk with the steward of the
convent in the neighbourhood, and as we returned, towards sunset, he

---

[7] See Metzger, *Text of the New Testament*, 35; P. W. Pestman, *The New Papyrological
Primer* (2nd ed.; Leiden: Brill, 1997).

begged me to take some refreshment with him in his cell. Scarcely had he entered the room, when, resuming our former subject of conversation, he said: "And I, too, have read a Septuagint" – i.e. a copy of the Greek translation made by the Seventy. And so saying, he took down from the corner of the room a bulky kind of volume, wrapped up in a red cloth, and laid it before me. I unrolled the cover, and discovered, to my great surprise, not only those very fragments which, fifteen years before, I had taken out of the basket,[8] but also other parts of the Old Testament, the New Testament complete, and, in addition, the Epistle of Barnabas and a part of the Shepherd of Hermas.[9]

As Tischendorf's reflections indicate, Codex Sinaiticus is a fourth-century uncial containing part of the Greek Old Testament (Septuagint), the entire NT, the Epistle of Barnabas, and parts of the Shepherd of Hermas. It is one of the most valuable manuscripts of the NT.[10] Codex Vaticanus (early fourth century) is also a very important uncial manuscript. In addition to their nicknames (e.g., "Codex Sinaiticus"), scholars use a shorthand system to refer to uncials. This shorthand system designates uncials by letters of the alphabet, or numbers prefixed with a zero (e.g., B = 03, C = 04, etc.).[11]

Sometime during the ninth century, minuscules – or manuscripts written in smaller, cursive characters – were developed. With an increased number of letters per page written in a faster style of handwriting, minuscules offered a more efficient approach to copying the NT. Thus from the ninth century forward, minuscule codices are found in greatest abundance. Designated by Arabic numerals, more than 2,800 minuscule manuscripts exist today.

Finally, citations from the NT once used as lessons on important days of the church calendar are also often used in the process of

---

[8] On a previous visit Tischendorf had rescued certain manuscript fragments from a basket full of papers valued as rubbish and, therefore, in use as kindling for the stove.

[9] See Constantin von Tischendorf, *When Were Our Gospels Written? An Argument by Constantine Tischendorf: With a Narrative of the Discovery of the Sinaitic Manuscript* (New York: American Tract Society, 1866).

[10] Metzger, *Text of the New Testament*, 45.

[11] See Appendix 1 of K. Aland et al., rev. and ed., *Novum Testamentum Graece* (27th ed.; Stuttgart: Deutsche Bibelstiftung, 1993), 80–1.

reconstructing the NT texts. Such citations are found in what are referred to as lectionaries – books containing a variety of scriptural citations appointed for worship on a given day or occasion. There are more than 2,280 lectionaries exhibiting both uncial and minuscule scripts. Scholars refer to lectionaries with a small letter "l" plus an Arabic numeral.

One final manuscript type complements those mentioned so far. As one might expect, Christian writers from the second to the tenth centuries often cited or alluded to NT passages. These citations offer valuable information about texts – perhaps now lost, but current in the time when, and in the location where, the Christian intellectual lived and worked. We refer to these passages as "patristic" or "late antique" citations.

Excluding these late antique citations, scholars thus have at their disposal for study a total of approximately 5,000 hand-copied Greek manuscripts of various parts of the NT dating from between the second century and the sixteenth century. Close evaluation of these manuscripts reveals important general similarities. These general similarities led to a system of manuscript classification by familial traits called text types. Two primary text types are clearly distinguishable. From the sixteenth until the nineteenth centuries, the first text type, represented by more than 800 Greek minuscules, was thought to represent the original NT. It was dubbed the Received Text, or in Latin, the *Textus Receptus*, and formed the basis for all printed editions of the Greek NT (and thus English translations) during this time. However, by the late nineteenth century, with the discovery of previously unknown and much older uncials and papyri, scholars acknowledged a second text type, referred to as the Alexandrian text type. Today both Protestants and Roman Catholics base their translations more on the Alexandrian type than on the Received Text.

Copying manuscripts by hand led to errors or variants. More than 200,000 variants can be identified in our more than 5,000 manuscripts. The most important problem for text critics is how to adjudicate among the many variants in order to arrive at a realistic approximation of an original NT text. One principle used by text critics for establishing the text is that variants that explain other variants constitute the best reading. That is, if one variant is explainable as an emendation – either an addition to or a subtraction from – of another variant, then the latter variant seems to reflect a prior stage of text transmission. Such decisions are made on the basis of external evidence (e.g., a manuscript's age, text type, or provenance) and internal evidence (e.g., a manuscript's diction, style, or characteristic ideas, including those of its copyist).

Once the complicated work of deciding upon a Greek text is complete, the task of translation is at hand. It is important to keep in mind that translations initiate another step away from the original texts, considerably compounding problems of interpretation. Translations today range from the more conservative (literal) to the more liberal (paraphrase). Text critics usually do not become involved in the work of modern language translation, leaving this important, separate task to others.[12]

Source Criticism

Source criticism analyzes texts for signs of the written sources on which they were based. Arriving at a satisfying text of the NT, what would we like to know next about the text to better understand it? We would probably like to know who wrote the text. We might also like to know the author's background, for example, when, where, for whom, on the basis of what, and why the text was written. We might like to know why a certain element was included, whether that element derives from a source, and whether that source was oral or written.

During the late nineteenth century, a German scholar by the name of Julius Wellhausen (1844–1918) developed a method for resolving some of these important literary–historical questions. Although

---

[12] Dynamic (active) equivalence and formal (passive/reflexive) equivalence are two different approaches to translation. Dynamic equivalence emphasizes readability, whereas formal equivalence emphasizes preserving original wording. Eugene A. Nida is credited with describing the principle of dynamic equivalence first (*Fascinated by Languages* [Amsterdam: J. Benjamins, 2003]).

known today in a wide variety of different applications, Wellhausen's theory dealt with the composition of the Pentateuch. This theory became known as the documentary hypothesis (DH). The documentary hypothesis proposed that the first five books of the Hebrew Bible (i.e., Genesis, Exodus, Leviticus, Numbers, and Deuteronomy) represent a mixture of four originally independent sources. These sources with the approximate dates of their composition were: (1) J, or Jahwist source (*ca.* 950 B.C.E.) in the southern kingdom of Judah noted, in part, for its use of the name, "YHWH" or "Yahweh" for God (*Yahweh* begins with the letter "J" in German); (2) E, or Elohist source (*ca.* 850 B.C.E.) in the northern kingdom of Israel noted, in part, for its use of the name, "Elohim" for God; (3) D, or Deuteronomist source (*ca.* 621 B.C.E.) in Jerusalem, possibly during a religious reform; and (4) P, or Priestly source (*ca.* 450 B.C.E.) by Aaronid priests. Wellhausen dubbed the person responsible for combining the sources into the final Pentateuch "R" for Redactor, speculating that he might have been the well-known figure Ezra.[13]

With this important theory, Wellhausen pioneered the method known as source criticism. It is a method used to analyze the written sources behind the texts as reconstructed by textual critics. For example, it is frequently observed that the Gospels of Matthew, Mark, and Luke share a similar outline and content. If these three Gospels are placed in parallel columns next to one another these similarities can be easily seen. Such a comparison is commonly known as a "synopsis," eliciting the qualifier "synoptic" as a reference for these Gospels. The problem of the relationships among these Gospels is thus referred to as the "Synoptic Problem." Solutions to the Synoptic Problem help scholars date the Gospels. For example, because Matthew and Mark most often agree against Luke, and Mark and Luke agree against Matthew, but Matthew and Luke do not agree against Mark, most scholars believe that Mark was a source for both Matthew and Luke.

---

[13] See John H. Hayes and J. Maxwell Miller, eds., *Israelite and Judaean History* (3rd ed.; London: SCM, 1990) 61–4; Julius Wellhausen, *Prolegomena to the History of Ancient Israel* (Atlanta: Scholars Press, 1994 [1885]).

Furthermore, the Gospel of Mark is the shortest of the three Gospels (even if on occasion its version of a given passage is slightly longer). Source critics ask the question: Is it likely that the author of Mark omitted major sections from his source (imagining for the moment that Mark used Matthew as a source) while moderately expanding the few stories he took over? Is it not more plausible that the authors of Matthew and Luke shortened their versions of various passages in Mark to make room for other important sources either known or unknown to Mark? Moreover, Matthew and Luke refine the style, improve the grammar, and cut repetitious materials from Mark. It seems to most scholars more historically probable that a text would have been improved, polished, clarified, and expanded, rather than the other way around. Thus, a majority of scholars today think that the anonymous authors of the Gospels of Matthew and Luke used Mark as their common source. This theory is known as Markan priority. Markan priority attempts to explain why passages in Matthew, Luke, or both agree with Mark. It does not, however, explain parallel material in Matthew and Luke not found in Mark or traditions in Matthew and Luke only. I will address the former question first.

How do scholars explain parallel material in Matthew and Luke not found in Mark? Unless Matthew had Luke or vice versa, which seems in principle unlikely given (presumed) shared reliance on Mark, how should scholars account for verbatim agreement between Matthew and Luke not found in Mark? The most prevalent solution is that these verses came from a written source that has not survived apart from its incorporation in these texts. Since the late nineteenth century this hypothetical source has been referred to as "Q" from the German word, *Quelle* meaning "source."[14] Q is readily identifiable in a synopsis by scanning for parallel passages in Matthew and Luke not in Mark. The material amounts to around sixty-eight passages, less than a quarter of the total of either Gospel. It is distributed evenly throughout

---

[14] See Kurt Aland, ed., *Synopsis Quattuor Evangeliorum* (Stuttgart: Deutsche Bibelgesellschaft, 1996); James M. Robinson et al., *The Critical Edition of Q* (Hermeneia; Minneapolis, Minn.: Fortress, 2000).

both Matthew and Luke.[15] The material is almost exclusively sayings. For ease of reference, and because most scholars think Q's order is better preserved by Luke, it is customary to designate Q passages with Lukan versification preceded by the letter Q (i.e., Q 4:3–8 = Luke 4:3–8 = Matt 3:3–10). As a collection of sayings, Q resembles somewhat the Gospel of Thomas, discovered in Nag Hammadi, Egypt, in 1945. However, it has been pointed out that the sayings in the Gospel of Thomas possess quotation formulae attributing each one to Jesus, whereas Q's sayings lack such formulae.

Finally, numerous passages in Matthew and Luke are found in either one or the other Gospel exclusively. Like the passages from Mark and Q, these sections may also represent other sources, either written or oral. Today scholars designate this group of materials collectively as *Sondergut* (German: "special materials"). It is significant that roughly one-third of the Gospel of Luke is comprised of material peculiar to this Gospel.

Thus, the simplest and most widely held "solution"[16] to the Synoptic Problem is that Matthew and Luke relied primarily on two written sources, Mark and Q. This solution is referred to as the two-source hypothesis. Although this hypothesis represented scholarly consensus throughout the twentieth century and up to the present, research harbors uncertainty perhaps in an increasing amount today. At least four alternative solutions exist. The first and best known is the Griesbach or two-gospel hypothesis.[17] This proposal, advocated by

---

[15] In Matthew, Q appears in the five great speeches of Jesus (Matt 5–7, 10, 13, 18, 24–25). In Luke Q appears in five sections that alternate with sections from Mark (from Mark: Luke 3:1–6:1; from Q: Luke 6:20–8:3; from Mark: 8:4–9:50; from Q: Luke 9:51–18:14; from Mark: Luke 18:15–24:11). However, in Luke, the greatest portion of Q occurs in the so-called Travel Narrative (Luke 9:51–18:14).

[16] It is not really a solution, but a common deduction. The language of "solution" results from prior reference to the issue at hand as a "problem" (e.g., "the Synoptic Problem").

[17] Often traced to Johann Jakob Griesbach (1745–1812), for whom Matthew was the first written Gospel. Johann J. Griesbach, *Commentatio qua Marci evangelium totum e Matthaei et Lucae commentariis decerptum esse monstratur* (Jena, 1789/90); printed in *Commentationes theologicae* (ed. J. C. Velthausen et al.; Leipzig, 1794) 1.360 ff. See also J. B. Orchard, ed., *A Synopsis of the Four Gospels: In Greek: Arranged according to the Two-Gospel-Hypothesis* (Göttingen: Vandenhoeck & Ruprecht, 1983).

W. R. Farmer,[18] puts forward that Matthew and Luke were composed before Mark, dispensing with the Q hypothesis altogether.[19] According to Farmer and others, the author of Matthew wrote first, the author of Luke next (borrowing from Matthew and elsewhere), and the author of Mark last (compiling the common materials between Matthew and Luke and adding a small number of other traditions). One of the most compelling pieces of support for this position is the testimony of late antique authors. Clement of Alexandria (150–211/216 C.E.), for example, held that the Gospels with genealogies were written first (Eusebius, *Hist. eccl.* 6.14.5–7). Augustine too assumed Matthew was written first, followed by Luke, which was, in turn, followed by Mark (*De Consensu Evangelistarum* 4.10, 11).

Other theories about the interrelationship of the synoptic Gospels admit greater complexity in the evangelists' process of composition. The second alternative, known as the multiple-stage hypothesis and advocated by M. É Boismard, proposes that preliminary versions of the Synoptics and Q began the tradition simultaneously. Intermediate versions of Mark and Matthew were made first. Then a preliminary version of Luke was written, influenced by the intermediate version of Mark and incorporating Q. Finally, the intermediate version of Mark influenced the final versions of Matthew and Luke, whereas it was itself influenced by the preliminary version of Luke and the intermediate version of Matthew. Mark is thus in some way reliant on Matthew and Luke, whereas Matthew and Luke are also reliant on a preliminary version of Mark. Furthermore, Matthew and Luke used Q.[20]

---

[18] For an important collection of essays, including one by W. R. Farmer, see David L. Dungan, ed., *The Interrelations of the Gospels* (BETL 95; Leuven: Leuven University Press, 1990), 125–230.

[19] On the rejection of Q see, e.g., Austin Farrar, "On Dispensing with Q," in *Studies in the Gospels: Essays in Memory of R. H. Lightfoot* (ed. D. E. Nineham; Oxford: Blackwell, 1955); Mark Goodacre, "Beyond the Q Impasse or Down a Blind Alley," *JSNT* 76 (1999): 33–52. One claim that, if proven, might be persuasive is that Matthew and Luke follow Mark with less precision than do Q materials, implying that Q materials are more likely to have been transferred directly (from Matthew to Luke or vice versa) than mediated by a source.

[20] This summary comes from Schnelle, *History and Theology*, 177.

A third alternative, advocated by M. D. Goulder, attempts to prove that Luke knew and cited Matthew. In Goulder's opinion, Q never existed. Rather, around 90 C.E., the author of Luke-Acts composed his first *logos* by combining Matthew and Mark for Gentile churches. "Special L" simply builds on materials first available in the Gospel of Matthew.

The fourth alternative, advocated by Bo Reicke, is a variation on the oral tradition hypothesis. It deemphasizes written sources, rather describing triple tradition agreements as the result of oral traditions known to all three.[21]

No theory provides a wholly adequate solution to the Synoptic Problem. Rather, every new hypothesis brings with it new difficulties. That said, the two-source hypothesis still offers the best explanation of the most data. For this reason, it maintains the most support today.

Form Criticism

Form criticism is a method of biblical criticism that classifies units of scripture according to literary patterns and attempts to trace each unit to its historical context in a phase of oral (usually prior to written) transmission. Hermann Gunkel developed the method for study of the Jewish Scriptures.[22] Martin Noth, Gerhard von Rad, and other scholars used it to supplement Wellhausen's documentary hypothesis (see previous). Later, Karl Ludwig Schmidt, Martin Dibelius, Rudolf Bultmann, and others applied it with much success to the NT Gospels.[23]

The theory is founded on the assumption that, in addition to written sources, early Christians circulated oral traditions often thought to have preceded known written ones. These oral traditions may have

---

[21] Bo Reicke, "Die Entstehungsverhältnisse der synoptischen Evangelien," in *ANRW* 252 (1984): 1758–91; idem, *The Roots of the Synoptic Gospels* (Philadelphia: Fortress, 1986).

[22] H. Gunkel, *The Legends of Genesis* (Chicago: Open Court, 1901; reprinted with an introduction by W. F. Albright, New York: Schocken, 1964). See Hayes and Miller, eds., *Israelite and Judaean History*, 133–35.

[23] See William Baird, *History of New Testament Research*, vol. 1: *From Deism to Tübingen* (Minneapolis, Minn.: Fortress, 1992).

surpassed written traditions in value. For example, Papias, Bishop of Hierapolis (70/75–163 C.E.), once wrote: "For I did not suppose that information from books would help me so much as the word of a living and surviving voice" (Eusebius, *Hist. eccl.*, 3.39 [LCL]). Recognition of this importance of oral traditions among early Christians led German NT critics to study the phenomenon by means of our written texts.

How were oral traditions studied in written texts? The early form critics were primarily interested in three matters. First, they were interested in small, isolated, individual units of text known as pericopes (Greek: *peri* + *kopē*, "a cutting around"; from *koptein* "to cut"). Such units may represent stories, sayings, and hymns. A more detailed list includes aphorisms, parables, allegories, anecdotes, miracle stories, creeds, confessions, and prayers. These units are analyzed apart from their literary context often through comparison with similar forms.

Second, early form critics studied the socioreligious context of a given form. This context was referred to as the form's *Sitz im Leben* (German: "setting in life"). Settings-in-life included exposition, exhortation, and other expressions of worship. Each is a historical context in which a form can be seen to have functioned prior to its incorporation in a written context. These settings are understood in relation to reconstructed religious environments of early Christians.

Finally, form critics were interested in history – that is, in the evolution of a form through time in a series of gradually shifting settings. As both the settings, and thus functions, of forms changed over time, scholars presume that the forms changed – sometimes more, sometimes less subtly – too. For example, most scholars think that the parables attributed to Jesus were first told to challenge accepted religious and social attitudes. Later, however, they were understood as allegories offering religious teaching such as moral advice. In this process, the content of the parable may have been adapted to clarify its new implications (e.g., Mark 2:5b–10a). Like sources, therefore, form critics assume that simpler forms matured into more complex ones.

Close examination of such development is thought to expose stages of accretion among oral traditions.

Today form criticism has taken a new direction in the work of German scholar Klaus Berger.[24] Berger espouses a *wirkungsgeschtliche* or history-of-effects hermeneutic, an attempt to link the reception, effect, or impact of a given NT text on Christian communities with its form and content. A text's reception – at once a measurable and immeasurable effect – is, for Berger, the result of its rhetorical strategy. Berger's discussion of the rhetorical aspects of a text forges a connection between his version of form criticism and rhetorical criticism, as we will see in the following.

Redaction Criticism

Redaction criticism seeks to understand the reformulation of traditions, both written (source) and oral (form), for new applications. On an analogy with a pearl necklace, if the forms are pearls, redaction is the string. In his commentary on the Gospel of Mark (1956), Willi Marxsen coined the term *Redaktionsgeschichte* (English: "Redaction Criticism") to refer to a method of studying the NT that investigates the way that biblical writers reformulated their sources to create their own account.[25] Redaction criticism assumes that writers of the NT books, although they may have relied on sources, more than merely copied. Rather, in their writings, these authors put forth their own new and important views. Redaction criticism studies how, for example, the authors of Matthew and Luke modified Mark, Q, and other unspecified written and oral materials available to them. The changes made to

---

[24] See Klaus Berger, *Formen und Gattungen im Neuen Testament* (Stuttgart: Uni-Taschenbücher, 2005); idem, "Rhetorical Criticism, New Form Criticism, and New Testament Hermenetics," in *Rhetoric and the New Testament: Essays from the 1992 Heidelberg Conference* (ed. Stanley E. Porter and Thomas H. Olbricht; Sheffield: Sheffield Academic Press, 1993), 390–96; idem, "Wirkungsgeschichtliche Hermeneutik," in *Exegeses des Neuen Testaments* (ed. Klaus Berger; Heidelberg: Quelle & Meyer, 1984).

[25] Willi Marxsen, *Mark the Evangelist: Studies on the Redaction History of the Gospel* (3rd ed.; Nashville, Tenn.: Abingdon, 1969).

their sources in both style and emphasis reveal a redactor's prejudices and predilections, informing us about these otherwise unknown first-century individuals.

Rhetorical Criticism

Rhetorical criticism identifies ancient rhetorical forms and figures in NT texts as a means of better understanding a text's argument. Rhetorical criticism is a subspecies of the historical–critical method. Today this method takes two different forms. One form of rhetorical criticism – ancient rhetorical criticism – has roots in the eighteenth century and bears much in common with traditional form criticism. Its aim is to identify and analyze the use of ancient rhetorical forms and figures in early Christian texts. A second form of rhetorical criticism is interested in analyzing early Christian texts according to principles of modern rhetoric. Because early Christian texts are premodern, however, many historians reject the application of modern categories of research. In contrast, they insist that investigations of the rhetoric of an ancient text must be made on ancient terms. Despite certain resemblances to emphases of modern rhetoric (e.g., argumentation, text-intentionality, the historical and social contexts of the composition, and stylistic features that facilitate a given historian's aim),[26] the arguments of ancient rhetorical criticism are based on ancient sources alone,[27] and any lack of clarity with regard to method is attributable to the complexities of discerning the argumentative techniques of ancient texts rather than to an application of anachronistic systems of thought to them. In sum, whereas certain scholars insist on analyzing ancient sources on the terms of ancient rhetoric (e.g., Quintilian), other scholars expand this standard, permitting analysis of ancient sources on the terms of modern rhetoric either alone or combined

---

[26] Duane F. Watson and Alan J. Hauser, *Rhetorical Criticism of the Bible: A Comprehensive Bibliography with Notes on History and Method* (Leiden: Brill, 1993), 114.

[27] Margaret M. Mitchell, *Paul and the Rhetoric of Reconciliation: An Exegetical Investigation of the Language and Composition of 1 Corinthians* (Louisville, Ky.: Westminster John Knox, 1991), 7.

with analysis based on the ancient sources. Although to the former group the latter may be guilty of anachronism, it is also true that later cultures may perceive things in earlier cultures that early cultures were unable to see in themselves, necessitating the terms of the later cultures (unknown to the earlier culture) for their elucidation. In the end, it is probably best that if modern rhetoric is deployed either alone or in combination with ancient rhetoric, clear warrant is provided for its use.

Focusing on ancient rhetorical criticism, this historical–critical method flowered in the 1980s after the publication of Hans Dieter Betz's commentary on Galatians.[28] In this commentary, Betz argues that, although Galatians bears clear indications of epistolary genre, its body possesses the form and figures of an ancient deliberative speech, thereby disposing the letter well to analysis on the terms of ancient rhetoric – that is, the ancient art of argument. Betz's method builds mainly on the form-critical approach. Like form critics, he sought to identify units or forms within NT texts. However, Betz sought specifically rhetorical (not general literary) forms and sought them not in the synoptic Gospels but in Paul's letter to the Galatians. Nevertheless, Betz's study commenced a phase of identifying rhetorical form and figures in early Christian literature, including the synoptic Gospels, that has hardly abated.

Social-Scientific Criticism

As noted previously, one of the three goals of the early form critics was to isolate the *Sitze im Leben* or socioreligious settings of oral traditions in use by early Christian communities. The settings they discovered, however, were primarily church-related. Hymns and prayers, for example, were most likely preserved through use in worship. Other social questions, beyond worship, nevertheless persist. Generally speaking, these questions are pursued in two different ways.

---

[28] Hans Dieter Betz, *Galatians: A Commentary on Paul's Letter to the Churches in Galatia* (Hermeneia; Philadelphia: Fortress, 1979).

The first and older way of addressing the social questions related to the early Christian texts was pioneered by scholars such as Robert M. Grant, John Gager, Abraham J. Malherbe, Wayne A. Meeks, Gerd Theissen, and other important scholars of Christian origins. Their interests in social history derived from an expanding view of early Christianity, a result of taking seriously extracanonical texts and perspectives, and acknowledging diverse opinions within the NT itself. A debt of gratitude is owed to this approach for insisting on the broadest possible scope of the NT historical context.[29]

In contrast, a younger generation of NT historians borrows models developed for understanding social arrangements of various modern demographic groups (e.g., Mormons in the twentieth century) in the hope of illuminating the ancient evidence about early Christians. Plugging information from ancient literary texts into a variety of different modern scientific models, it attempts to outline historical conditions and explain how they developed over time.[30] Unfortunately, not only are the models anachronistic, but as these social historians acknowledge, a serious paucity of data poses a near insurmountable difficulty to research. Supplementation with archaeological data does not surmount the difficulty. Our information about the early Christians is still too limited to make effective use of sociological models. Other modern sociological information, however, may be useful in analysis of ancient texts. For example, James A. Kelhoffer judiciously included body mass index estimates from modern nutritional science to help us better understand the diet of John the Baptist.[31] Kelhoffer's historical–critical method thus extends beyond the traditional tools of text-, source-, form-, redaction-, and socioscientific-critical methods to include observations from modern science. As with modern rhetoric, clear warrant justifies use.

[29] See Foreword by Margaret M. Mitchell to Robert M. Grant, *Augustus to Constantine: The Rise and Triumph of Christianity in the Roman World* (Louisville, Ky.: Westminster John Knox, 2004), xxii–xxv.

[30] See, e.g., Rodney Stark, *The Rise of Christianity: A Sociologist Reconsiders History* (Princeton, N.J.: Princeton University Press, 1996).

[31] See James A. Kelhoffer, *The Diet of John the Baptist: "Locusts and Wild Honey" in Synoptic and Patristic Tradition* (WUNT 176; Tübingen: Mohr Siebeck, 2005).

Archaeology

Although archaeology, both general material culture and manuscripts, is, strictly speaking, not a subspecies of the historical–critical method, it is mentioned here because it underlies the method. Two discoveries during the twentieth century have been of particular importance to the study of early Christianity. Both are well known. The first is the discovery of the Dead Sea Scrolls found in 1947 near Qumran by the Dead Sea. The Dead Sea Scrolls offer a wealth of information about a Jewish sect vital around the lifetimes of John the Baptist, Jesus, James, Peter, and Paul. Most scholars identify this sect with the Essenes. Evidently the group responsible for the sectarian documents underwent some form of social and/or political repression. Interestingly, like Christianity, it possessed rituals of ablution, celebrated a sacred meal with bread and wine, venerated a certain teacher, and held beliefs about a messiah or messiahs. In addition to numerous copies of the Jewish Scriptures, the fragments of the scrolls discovered in the caves near Qumran also contain prayers, songs of blessing, and instruction about how to live virtuously and avoid sin.[32]

Whereas the texts discovered at Qumran are Jewish, the texts of the Nag Hammadi Library, discovered in Egypt in 1945, contain Christian concepts and ideas as well.[33] Although many of these texts were new to scholars when they were discovered, some were known prior to their discovery at Nag Hammadi. Today all of the texts found at Nag Hammadi are referred to as "Gnostic." That said, it is clear to scholars that they represent a wide variety of beliefs and practices.[34]

---

[32] *The Dead Sea Scrolls Study Edition* (2 vols.; ed. Florentino García Martínez and Eibert J. C. Tigchelaar; Leiden: Brill, 1997–98). See, e.g., John J. Collins, *Apocalypticism in the Dead Sea Scrolls* (New York: Routledge, 1997); idem, *The Scepter and the Star: The Messiahs of the Dead Sea Scrolls and Other Ancient Literature* (ABRL; New York: Doubleday, 1995).

[33] James M. Robinson, ed., *The Nag Hammadi Library in English* (rev. ed.; San Francisco: Harper, 1990).

[34] See Michael Allen Williams, *Rethinking Gnosticism: An Argument for Dismantling a Dubious Category* (Princeton, N.J.: Princeton University Press, 1996).

Conclusion

The methods listed in this chapter – subspecies of the historical–critical approach – are not the only tools plied by NT interpreters today. A wide variety of other methods are applied regularly to the study of early Christian literature. Without attempting to summarize these other valuable approaches, it should be acknowledged here that the philosophical movement known generally as postmodernism has had a significant effect on biblical studies.[35] In short, if both the writing and reading of history are a purely subjective exercise, then any number of approaches may offer new and valid interpretations of NT texts. Although these points can and are being disputed, at the very least, it can be said that postmodernism has taught historical critics of all types that our method can be customized according to an individual practitioner's strengths and ideas. As noted previously, James Kelhoffer, a self-professing historical critic, included body mass index to interpret the diet of John the Baptist.[36] Such a customized permutation of the historical–critical method, unique to Kelhoffer, exemplifies just one of many historical–critical methods in use today, suggesting expanding possibilities for this most august interpretive strategy.

TEXTUAL ANALYSIS: LUKE 20:45–21:4

The Gospel of Luke and the Historical–Critical Method

Although historical critics would argue that their method is useful for any early Christian text, it is also true that it helps elucidate some texts better than others. The Gospel of Luke, I think scholars would agree, is particularly susceptible to study by means of the historical–critical

---

[35] See, e.g., John J. Collins, *The Bible after Babel: Historical Criticism in a Postmodern Age* (Grand Rapids, Mich.: Eerdmans, 2005); idem, *Encounters with Biblical Theology* (Minneapolis, Minn.: Fortress, 2005).

[36] See Kelhoffer, *Diet of John the Baptist.*

method for the following five reasons: (1) manuscript evidence lends itself well to examination by text criticism; (2) its careful deployment of Mark and Q allow us to study reliance on sources; (3) an emphasis on the teachings of Jesus helps scholars to trace forms in this Gospel; (4) reliance on sources also, in turn, reveals the author's hand where sources are either not in use or have been deliberately modified, providing an unusually rich source of information about the tendencies of the author as redactor; and (5) a wealth of materials, both sources and redaction, submits interesting social-scientific data analyzable via models.

Building on the background material in the first part of this chapter, I will now attempt to demonstrate the effectiveness of the historical–critical method in action on a single important passage in the Gospel of Luke. My critical analysis argues that Luke 20:45–21:4 came to the author of Luke-Acts in his version of the Gospel of Mark. By means of redaction, however, the passage was adapted to suit the author's own distinctive aims and purposes.

Exegesis

The New Revised Standard Version (NRSV) English translation of the passage commences our study of Luke 20:45–21:4.

Luke 20:45–47

[45] In the hearing of all the people he said to the disciples, [46] "Beware of the scribes, who like to walk around in long robes, and love to be greeted with respect in the marketplaces, and to have the best seats in the synagogues and places of honor at banquets. [47] They devour widows' houses and for the sake of appearance say long prayers. They will receive the greater condemnation."

Luke 21:1–4

[1] He looked up and saw rich people putting their gifts into the treasury; [2] he also saw a poor widow put in two small copper coins. [3] He said, "Truly I tell you, this poor widow has put in more than all of them; [4] for all

of them have contributed[37] out of their abundance, but she out of her poverty has put in all she had to live on."

Text Criticism

Two primary text-critical issues pertain to this passage. The first occurs in Luke 20:45 where the possessive pronoun "his" is left out of manuscripts B and D.[38] The second variant occurs in Luke 21:4. The words "of God" added to the phrase "threw in among the other gifts" (see n. 38) may be an explanation of the word "gifts" for Gentiles who, according to Bruce Metzger and Roger Omanson, "had never seen the γαζοφυλάκιον (*gazophulakion*, "treasury"; v. 1) in the temple at Jerusalem." Omanson recommends:

It will probably be best not to translate the text literally. The word δῶρα in this context may mean "offering" and the sense is "they were casting into [the treasury] their gifts [τὰ δῶρα]" or it may mean "offering-chest," that is, "they were casting [their offerings] into the offering-chest [εἰς τὰ δῶρα]."[39]

Source Criticism

Luke's Gospel begins with a statement suggesting his reliance on sources:

Since many have undertaken to set down an orderly account of the events that have been fulfilled among us, *just as they were handed on to us by those who from the beginning were eyewitnesses and servants of the word*, I too decided, after investigating everything carefully from the very first, to write an orderly account for you, most excellent Theophilus, so that you may know the truth concerning the things about which you have instructed. (1:1–4, NRSV; emphasis added)

---

[37] Literally: "threw in among the other gifts [of God]." See the discussion following.
[38] Roger L. Omanson, *A Textual Guide to the Greek New Testament* (Stuttgart: Deutsche Bibelgesellschaft, 2006), 145–6.
[39] Omanson, *Textual Guide*, 146. See also BDAG, 267.

Furthermore, Markan priority asserts that Luke's reliance on sources (see Synoptic Problem previously) included Mark. Although scholars must not jump too hastily to the conclusion that Luke's Mark was identical to ours, nevertheless, in the case of this passage, Luke's version of Mark is virtually identical. Integration of our passage by the author of the Gospel of Matthew with Q material (Matt 23:1–39; cf. Luke 11:37–54) suggests Luke's version was not deficient.

The passage (Luke 20:45–21:4) arises in the fourth and final block of Markan material in Luke: (1) Luke 3:1–6:19; (2) Luke 8:4–9:50; (3) Luke 18:15–43; and (4) Luke 19:28–21:38.[40] The fourth block constitutes a bridge between Jesus' arrival in Jerusalem (9:51–19:27) and his suffering, death (22:1–23:56), and resurrection (24:1–53). The block takes place in the temple in Jerusalem in both Mark (12:38–44) and Luke.[41] Source criticism, hence, is important for an accurate understanding of this passage by making readers aware that the author adopted this passage from Mark. Redaction criticism will pick up changes made to Mark by Luke, in this case, the passage's special role in its present context.

Form Criticism

Examined from a form-critical standpoint, the two sections comprising our passage are properly separated into Luke 20:45–47 and Luke 21:1–4.

The first section (Luke 20:45–47) resembles the woes pronounced on the scribes and Pharisees from Q (Luke 11:43, 46, 52, 42, 39, 44, 47; cf. Matt. 23:4, 6, 13, 23, 25, 27, 29). It is possible that Mark's single denunciation of the scribes was later amplified into this collection of woes in Luke and Matthew (i.e., Q).[42] Bultmann categorized this first section as a prophetic/apocalyptic saying and recommends we stay alert to the

---

[40] See previous n. 15. In other words, our passage was not left out of Luke as in the so-called Great Omission (of Mark 6:45–8:26).

[41] Jesus enters the temple in Mark 12:35, but in Luke 20:1 (cf. 19:45). See Adela Yarbro Collins, *Mark: A Commentary* (Hermeneia; Minneapolis, Minn.: Fortress, 2007).

[42] In Matt 23:1, 6, Markan material is combined with Q and Special M forming a longer list of woes against the Pharisees.

possibility of such a tradition's growth,[43] that is, the possibility that Mark's individual saying provided a basis for the series of woes in Q. For Bultmann, prophetic/apocalyptic sayings are classified as dominical sayings with wisdom sayings and laws or community regulations.[44] Chief elements of the category of dominical sayings indicate, according to Bultmann, that they originated not in a Hellenistic but an Aramaic context.[45] The sayings are thus Jewish traditions adapted to a *Sitz im Leben* of teaching contexts in the early church.[46] This saying is also considered, to use Bultmann's terminology, minatory, that is, a threatening warning by Jesus to his disciples about the hypocritical behavior of certain scribes.[47]

Bultmann categorizes the second saying as a biographical apophthegm.[48] In Bultmann's form-critical system, an apophthegm (a term from Greek literature) is a unit of text containing "sayings of Jesus set in a brief context."[49] The *Sitz im Leben* of apophthegms is, according to Bultmann, within discussions between the early church and its opponents.[50] However, as Adela Yarbro Collins points out in her commentary on Mark, this passage "is not biographical in the strict sense, since it is an ideal scene that discusses 'the proper standard for judging a sacrifice' for the benefit of the church."[51] In this passage, both Mark and Luke depict Jesus as sitting in the outer court of the temple watching people put money in a collection box either as they enter or exit.[52] At one point, some rich people deposit money, after which

---

[43] Rudolf Bultmann, *History of the Synoptic Tradition* (New York: Harper & Row, 1963), 113–14; cf. Martin Dibelius, *From Tradition to Gospel* (New York: Charles Scribner's Sons, 1935), 236–37.
[44] Bultmann, *History of the Synoptic Tradition*, 69. Skepticism exists around this category of Bultmann's, in particular for its lack of an ancient equivalent.
[45] Bultmann, *History of the Synoptic Tradition*, 166.
[46] Bultmann, *History of the Synoptic Tradition*, 126.
[47] Bultmann, *History of the Synoptic Tradition*, 111. So also Joseph A. Fitzmyer, *The Gospel According to Luke* (2 vols; AB 28–28A; Garden City, N.Y.: Doubleday, 1981–5), 2:1316–17.
[48] Bultmann, *History of the Synoptic Tradition*, 32–3, 56–7.
[49] Bultmann, *History of the Synoptic Tradition*, 11.
[50] Bultmann, *History of the Synoptic Tradition*, 41.
[51] Collins, *Mark*, 587.
[52] Collins, *Mark*, 588.

a poor widow follows, offering only two lepta (small copper coins).[53] Observing this scene, Jesus makes the comment that constitutes our second section. This comment is analyzed in greater detail in the section on rhetorical criticism following.

Redaction Criticism

Retaining the bipartite division of our passage, we begin our discussion of the redaction–critical issue of our passage with Luke 20:45–47. As far as we can tell, the author changes very little from his Markan source in Luke 20:45–47. To be precise, the author makes only three minor modifications: (1) he adds v. 45 as an introduction; (2) he uses a genitive absolute to avoid the parataxis – the juxtaposition of syntactic units next to each other without the insertion of a conjunction, as in Mark 12:37c; and (3) he substitutes προσέχω (*prosechō*, "give heed") for βλέπω (*blepō*, "beware") in v. 46. Other than these very minor changes, the author follows Mark in this first section of our passage word for word.[54]

Similarly, few changes are made from Mark in the second section of our passage (Luke 21:14). In v. 1 the author eliminates the situation of Jesus sitting down outside the temple and watching rich people make generous contributions. It should be pointed out, however, that Matthew omits this episode from his narrative as well. The rest of the minor changes made to Mark's text by Luke are succinctly summarized by commentator Joseph Fitzmyer:

---

[53] Collins explains, "The copper lepton was the smallest Greek coin denomination. The denomination 'lepton' occurs in the papyri from Nahal Hever. The documents also mention a Nabatean coin denomination called the *melaina*, which was a silver coin. One such coin was worth more than fifty-eight lepta. A *melaina* was worth less than a denarius. The name λεπτόν (*novmisma*) ("small coin") was used for whatever was the smallest denomination of coins in the Syrian-Nabatean region. Under Herod the Great and after 6 c.e., the smallest coin minted in Judea was the *perutah* or *prutah*. Since it was the smallest coin in circulation, it could be called a 'lepton'" (*Mark*, 589). Collins concludes that Mark's inclusion of lepta make it more likely it was written in an eastern province (*Mark*, 589).

[54] Fitzmyer, *Luke*, 2:1316.

Verses 2–4 follow the Marcan form of the episode, but Luke abridges them by eliminating the Latinism *kodrantes*... and the summoning of the disciples (cf. 20:45). Luke also uses a poetic word *penichra*, "poor, needy," instead of Mark's more ordinary work *ptoche*, "beggarly, poor," in his initial description of the widow (v. 2), only to revert to the latter in Jesus' comment itself (v. 3), as he follows his source. In v. 4 he slightly improves the Greek style.[55]

Redaction, however, does not only amount to adaptations of the pericope from its source. It also involves placement of the source in the new literary setting, including both position and relevance. As noted previously, in both Mark and Luke this passage forms a bridge between Jesus' arrival in Jerusalem (9:51–19:27) and his suffering, death (22:1–23:56), and resurrection (24:1–53). A key difference between the two Gospels with respect to this passage is the importance of the arrival in Jerusalem – and specifically at the temple – in Luke over and against Mark. The Gospel of Luke possesses a very clear emphasis on Jerusalem not present in Mark. First, the Gospel begins with two stories of Jesus visiting Jerusalem as a child (Luke 2:22–40, 41–51). Then, in the middle of the Gospel, from Luke 9:51–19:27, in what has come to be called Luke's "Travel Narrative," the author describes Jesus as making slow progress toward Jerusalem. Throughout this special section of narrative the author repeatedly reminds us that Jesus is making his way toward Jerusalem (9:51, 53; 13:22, 33; 17:11; 18:31; 19:11, 28, 41). When Jesus finally arrives in Jerusalem he weeps over it (19:41–44), probably suggesting his frustrated devotion to a city known for rejecting legitimate prophets. This weeping pericope is "Special L" material, not found in Mark or Matthew. As such, it seems to represent one of the author's unique emphases.

Our pericope is a rare section in the Gospels describing Jesus' ministry in Jerusalem prior to his arrest (Luke 19:28–21:38). After our section, the Gospel narrates Jesus' passion – or the events leading up to and following his death. After Jesus is killed, whereas in Mark and Matthew figures tell those searching for Jesus' body that he has

---

[55] Fitzmyer, *Luke*, 2: 1320.

gone ahead to Galilee (cf. Mark 14:28; 16:7; Matt 28:7), in Luke all resurrection appearances occur in and around Jerusalem (Luke 24:1–43; cf. Matt 28:16–20). Moreover, in Luke, when Jesus appears to his disciples, he instructs them to remain in Jerusalem (Luke 24:49; cf. also Acts 1:4). This interest in Jerusalem on the part of the author even persists in Acts. Acts 1–2 characterize this city as the place from which the entire Christian movement spreads. Also, in Acts 15, Jerusalem serves as the location of the first important early church council.[56]

Furthermore, the temple in Jerusalem has special importance in this Gospel. Not only does the Gospel begin in the temple, but Acts – the "second volume" of Luke's history – begins there as well. Although both Jerusalem and the temple are adopted as the setting of our particular passage from Mark 12:35–44 (it is not until Mark 13:1 that Jesus comes out of the temple to predict its demise), their distinctive emphasis in the Gospel of Luke overall gives our passage special value in this secondary literary setting. The author of the Gospel of Luke did not adopt any feature from his sources without carefully considering its relevance in his own version of the events. The author of the Gospel of Luke used sources judiciously. We know from what is commonly referred to as the "Great Omission," Luke's omission of Mark 6:45–8:26,[57] that where the author of Luke did not see value in a given pericope or section of pericopes, he did not hesitate to excise them. With this fact in mind, our passage (Luke 20:45–21:4) takes on special importance in the Gospel of Luke as among Jesus' final teachings in the great city in its great temple. Our passage represents in this important context the last teachings of Jesus on matters other than those pertaining to his capture, arrest, and murder. As such, our passage constitutes an epitome of his teaching overall. In this regard, it is significant that in references to scribes in preceding episodes in Luke, Jesus is not always critical. His final assessment of them is, however, quite negative.[58]

---

[56] See Powell, *Fortress Introduction to the Gospels*, 91–2.
[57] Cf. also Luke's "little omission" of Mark 9:41–10:12.
[58] So Fitzmyer, *Luke*, 2:1317.

We might also add to the importance placed on Jerusalem and the temple by the author of Luke a similar social-scientific critical emphasis on women. Although common to Mark's text as well, the key concept in our passage is the widow, the very expression "widow" acting as a catchword between the two sections of the passage: Speech against the Pharisees and Scribes (Luke 20:45–47) and the Widow's Mite (Luke 21:1–4). Although this link originates in Mark, it picks up on a Lukan tendency to accentuate the role of women. For example, the infancy narrative in Luke 1–2 focuses on the role of Mary rather than Joseph as in Matthew (Luke 1:26–56; Matt 1:18–25). Also, only Luke mentions Elizabeth, the mother of John the Baptist (1:24–25, 41–55), and Anna, the prophetess (2:36–38). Additional reports about women unique to Luke include Jesus' raising the widow's son at Nain (7:11–17), Jesus' forgiveness of the sinful woman in the city (7:36–50), Jesus' visit to Martha and Mary (10:38–42), and that Jesus' ministry was financially supported by women (8:1–3).[59] In conclusion, redaction criticism reveals pronounced emphases on Jerusalem, the temple, and women in the Gospel of Luke that give our passage a particularly significant role in this secondary context.

Rhetorical–Critical Issues

In treating rhetorical-critical issues, it is again preferable to retain a bipartite division of the pericope into Saying no. 1 (Luke 20:45–47) and Saying no. 2 (Luke 21:1–4). Although the foci of a given rhetorical–critical reading can be diverse (e.g., analyzing the passages in the context of the entire book or canon), this presentation takes up an analysis in terms of ancient rhetoric. Such an approach helps us to understand the author's argumentative strategy at this point in his composition. A rhetorical interpretive framework is to be preferred to others for its historical, literary, and cultural simultaneity with our text. That rhetoric is clearly in evidence not just elsewhere in the NT

---

[59] Powell, *Fortress Introduction to the Gospels*, 93.

but in many different sections of Luke-Acts lends credence to the postulate of its presence in our short section.

Saying no. 1 (Luke 20:45–47): After v. 45, which serves an introductory role, the saying is divided into five parts:

I. Eschatological warning
   A. Imperative: "Beware of the scribes" because...
      i. Six justifications for the warning:
         a. Four positive actions
           1. [they] "like to walk around in long robes"
           2. [they] "love to be greeted with respect in the market places"
           3. [they love] "to have the best seats in the synagogues"
           4. [they love to have] "the places of honor at banquets"
         b. Two negative actions
           5. [they] "devour widow's houses"
           6. [they] ("for the sake of appearance") "say long prayers"
   B. Predicted eschatological result: "They will receive the greater condemnation."

Saying no. 2 (Luke 21:1–4): Verses 1 and 2 are introductory. Together they form an ἀντίθεσις[60] (*antithesis*), a statement with two contrasting phrases that balance each other. They also offer the biographical context for the subsequent saying.

II. Biographical setting: "He [Jesus] looked up and saw..."
   A. Introductory ἀντίθεσις ("antithesis"): Rich people's *versus* poor individual's contributions to temple treasury
      i. "Rich people putting their contributions into the [temple] treasury"
      ii. "A poor widow put in two small copper coins"

---

[60] See R. Dean Anderson Jr., *Glossary of Greek Rhetorical Terms* (Leuven: Peeters, 2000), 21–2.

III. Apophthegmatic saying (παράδοχον or "paradox")[61]:
   A. Observation in form of παράδοχον:
       i. Introductory formula: "Truly I tell you . . . "[62]
       ii. Saying (content): "This poor widow has put in more than all of them."
   B. Παράδοχον explained using categories of antithesis:
       i. "For" signifies explanation
       ii. Rich (pl.): "all of them have contributed out of their abundance"
       iii. Contrasting conjunction: "but"
       iv. Widow (sg.): "she out of her poverty has put in all she had to live on."

The catchword "widow" links the second passage to the first. This bonding derives from Mark's version of the passage. The initial statement that the poor widow "has put in more than all of them" is, of course, not correct from a common sense, literal, or economic standpoint. The woman did not, in fact, put in more money than the other donors.

The second statement, however, explains how the first statement makes sense. It does so by correcting the assumption that economic value has the same pride of place in teaching about the kingdom of God as it does in life outside of the kingdom. In contrast, it claims that pride of place in the kingdom goes to any willing to sacrifice their life. The widow gave only two small copper coins, but these two coins represent, as the text specifies, her entire personal livelihood.[63] The widow gave her life sustenance. In doing so, she demonstrated what

---

[61] A "paradox" is a figure of speech that offers a contrast often for the purpose of surprise. See Anderson, *Glossary*, 88. Anderson's assimilation of the ancient rhetorical sources on this concept clarifies its primary usage as one of "surprise" (Demetrius, *Eloc.* 152–53) and "jesting" (Cicero, *de Orat.* 2.255, 284–85; Quint. *Inst.* 6.3.84; cf. also 6.3.24).

[62] An important, possibly prophetic statement; cf. Mark 3:28; 8:12; 9:1, 41; 10:15, 29; 11:23. See Collins, *Mark*, 589–90.

[63] "The word translated as livelihood here is βίος, which also has the meaning 'life,' in the sense of 'life and activity associated with it'" (Collins, *Mark*, 590).

is for the Jesus movement (at least according to this passage) a more primary value than economic welfare. She demonstrated the kingdom value of self-sacrifice. As Collins points out with regard to this passage in Mark, although the scribes know the greatest commandment (Deut 6:5), "And you shall love the Lord your God with your whole heart and with your whole life and with your whole mind and with your whole strength," only the widow fulfills it.[64] As in Mark (12:29–30; 12:32–33), in Luke this commandment is cited prior to our passage (Luke 10:27). Another interpretation of this passage, similar to that offered by Collins, is that the widow's offering is predicated on trust that God will reward the fulfillment of religious duties. The more wealthy people (implicitly here: the scribes) possess the same motive as the widow, but lack her trust.

However, it is also possible for the Markan, and thus Lukan, passage to be interpreted as words of criticism rather than approval for the widow. Joseph Fitzmyer argues that in Mark 7:10–13 Jesus advocates human needs over religious obligations, if they conflict.[65] Although Mark 7:10–13 is absent from Luke, Jesus' teaching about healing on the Sabbath (Mark 3:1–5; cf. Luke 6:6–11) makes the same point. Moreover, the first half of our passage condemns scribes for "devouring the estates of widows." In the argument of A. G. Wright on the widow in Mark 12:42/Luke 21:2: "Her religious thinking has accomplished the very thing that the scribes were accused of doing."[66] Therefore, it is also possible to conclude about this passage that Jesus is no happier about the widow than he was about the scribes. On his final day of open-air preaching in and around the temple before his betrayal and arrest, he not only turns over its tables (Mark 11:15–17; Luke 19:45–46), but condemns both its leaders (scribes: Mark 12:38–40; Luke 20:45–47) and followers (rich and poor alike: Mark 12:41–44; Luke 21:1–4) before predicting its destruction (Mark 13:1–2; Luke 21:5–6).

---

[64] Collins, *Mark*, 590.
[65] Fitzmyer, *Luke*, 2:1321.
[66] A. G. Wright, "The Widow's Mites: Praise or Lament? A Matter of Context," *CBQ* 44 (1982): 262.

CONCLUSION

Application of the historical–critical method – in it current subdisci-
plines of text, source, form, redaction, rhetorical, and social-scientific
criticisms – to Luke 20:45–21:4 demonstrates the effectiveness of the
method for eliciting meaning from ancient texts. Five contributions
stand out:

(1) The historical–critical method establishes the relative stability of
Luke 20:45–21:4. Text critics, through careful comparison of the
manuscript evidence, demonstrate relative agreement among
witnesses of this passage, although they acknowledge that the
witnesses may be at some remove from the original, either the
first oral or the first written, witness to the teaching.

(2) The historical–critical method demonstrates that the passage in
Luke stems from Mark, adopted (almost) verbatim from this
source. This observation informs us that the author esteemed
Mark as a credible, prior witness to the historical phenomena
he too wished to narrate. Mark was, however, not perfect. One
might say, "Worth rewriting!"

(3) Both form and redaction criticisms help us to divide our passage
into two separate pericopes, each likely to have been handed
down in oral tradition prior to their written form. The first
pericope contains a saying of Jesus, designated by Bultmann as
a dominical saying of the prophetic–apocalyptic type. Its *Sitz im
Leben* or "setting-in-life" is adoption of a Jewish form to Christian teaching. The second pericope contains what Bultmann
referred to as a biographical apophthegm, a saying placed in
a brief narrative context the primary purpose of which was to
stage the saying. The *Sitz im Leben* or historical context of this
saying was early church discussions.

(4) Although our passage in Luke closely resembles its parent
version in Mark, the historical–critical method has theo-
rized, by means of redaction criticism, a special purpose for
this pericope in Luke's Gospel. Redaction criticism highlights

important Lukan themes on which our passage touches, including Jerusalem, the temple, and women.

(5) Finally, the historical–critical method aptly analyzes our passage on the basis of ancient rhetorical categories. Such an analysis offers an interpretation of the passage featuring precise functions and intentions down to the individual word. A rhetorical–critical analysis of Luke 20:45–21:4 draws attention to its use of categories such as ἀντίθεσις (*antithesis*) and παράδοχον (*paradoxon*). It also, together with source and redaction criticism, compares other sayings in the Gospel of Luke to reveal, in the case of the widow's mite saying, competing implications.

Although individual subspecies of the historical–critical method evolved separately (sometimes consecutively, building on each other), today they are best used together. Whereas individually they may miss the mark by overemphasizing a certain aspect of a text, such as its wholesale adoption from a source, together the individual methods offer an effective panoply of resources for exegesis. That said, the method still, in some cases, falls short. As critics have not been hesitant to point out, the historical–critical method fails to deal adequately with issues of race, class, gender, and other political effects evident in texts (whether history, myth, fiction, propaganda, or some combination). What is more, for nearly a century and a half, practitioners have, wittingly and unwittingly, espoused the scientific objectivity of the method. This claim is hopelessly unachievable on many levels, exacerbated by both the nature of the materials (i.e., ancient) and their claims. Today, as this volume demonstrates, most of these objections are dealt with through recourse to supplementary or alternative methods including Latino–Latina, feminist, reader response, and postcolonial. Nevertheless, much work remains to be done in bringing these diverse interpretations together in comprehensive yet cogent interpretations that benefit all, both practitioners and their audiences.

Finally, although typically taught and practiced as an effective means of interpreting biblical texts, the historical–critical method is also of use to other academic fields of research. One thinks first of its value for interpreting ancient nonbiblical religious texts. However, the method might also be successful with modern, nonreligious texts. Today the method is frequently the envy of disciplines, such as ancient Near Eastern studies, classics, English literature, and history.

At the same time, however, it is also true that some shun the method, not for the shortcomings noted previously that have been addressed by other methods (e.g., feminist, postcolonial), but on pious grounds. For such dissidents, an irony persists. By emphasizing the human production component of biblical texts, practitioners are accused of failing to appreciate their theological value. However, it was precisely the theological importance of the biblical texts that initially drove scholars as early as Erasmus to develop the method. I conclude, thus, that the powerful theological importance of the biblical texts that first elicited and often still compels their earnest and painstaking examination frequently identifies causes and meanings not at peace with the drive that first sought them.

3

↓

Feminist Criticism

Turid Karlsen Seim

Among feminist interpreters, the Gospel of Luke is contested ground. The interpretations are not only diverse but marked by contradiction. Early feminist studies on Luke were almost programmatically positive, looking for and calling forth the unusually large number of women who are mentioned in the text.[1] However, this was soon challenged by a far more critical evaluation maintaining that Luke represented a rhetorical strategy whereby women were restricted to silence and subservience.[2]

It is therefore no coincidence that the introduction to the volume on the Gospel of Luke in the series "A Feminist Companion" begins with two paragraphs, each representing an established feminist position on Luke, and the one contradicting the other. Some hold that "the Gospel of Luke celebrates women's discipleship, self-determination,

---

[1] E.g., Constance F. Parvey, "The Theology and Leadership of Women in the New Testament," in *Religion and Sexism* (ed. Rosemary Radford Ruether; New York: Simon and Schuster, 1974), 139–46; E. Jane Via, "Women in the Gospel of Luke," in *Women in the World's Religions: Past and Present* (ed. Ursula King; New York: Paragon, 1987), 38–55.

[2] Elisabeth Schüssler Fiorenza coined the term "the Lukan silence" and has maintained this position in all her early contributions, with greatest impact in her influential and by now classic monograph, *In Memory of Her: A Feminist Theological Reconstruction of Christian Origins* (New York: Crossroad, 1983). See also, for example, Elsa Tetlow, *Women and Ministry in the New Testament: Called to Serve* (New York: Paulist, 1980). It should be mentioned that Luke is being treated mostly as Luke-Acts, involving a discussion as to how the two volumes correlate; cf. Turid Karlsen Seim, *The Double Message: Patterns of Gender in Luke-Acts* (Edinburgh: T. & T. Clark, 1994), 3–6.

and leadership even as it heralds a reversal of systemic inequities," whereas others claim that "the Gospel of Luke threatens any attempt made by women, the poor or the disenfranchised to find a voice in either society or church. The narrative consistentsly depicts women in ancillary capacities. . . . Luke's gospel is a menacing text that retains and reinforces kyriarchal structures."[3] Interpreters do often disagree, but how are such extremely opposed positions, equally committed to the common cause of feminist criticism, possible in relation to the same source? Is a middle ground possible? Is a middle ground even desirable or required?

total nonsense politically motivated pitch

feminist criticism isn't a method, it's a rhetoric.

THE MULTIPLICITY OF FEMINIST CRITICISMS

Feminist criticism on Luke is a showcase for the observation that commitment to feminism does not lead to uniformity. The multiple and even contradictory readings of a single text may be taken to reflect the fact that feminism is itself a plurality of possible positions, "variously shaped by historical circumstances, political and theological allegiances, social identities, institutional locations, and intellectual interests."[4] Indeed, within feminist criticism we find an active interest in decentering the notion of a singular interpretation and, accordingly, in developing a strategy of multiple readings of the same passage, readings that calmly may be regarded as equally compelling.

Feminist criticism aims at uncovering power structures that keep women in place as "the other" and overcoming the marginalization of women and any cognition marked by androcentrism.[5] It is born out of

bull.

[3] Amy-Jill Levine with Marianne Blickenstaff, eds., *A Feminist Companion to Luke* (London: Sheffield Academic Press, 2002), 1. The terms kyriarchal and kyriocentric are drawn from Elisabeth Schüssler Fiorenza, *Rhetoric and Ethics: The Politics of Biblical Studies* (Minneapolis, Minn.: Fortress, 1999), ix.

[4] Anonymous, "Feminist and Womanist Criticism," in *The Postmodern Bible* (ed. Elizabeth A. Castelli, Stephen D. Moore, Gary A. Phillips, and Regina M. Schwarz; New Haven, Conn.: Yale University Press, 1995), 225–71, has this as its profile.

[5] Despite postmodern complaints that terms such a patriarchy and androcentrism are naïve or at least imprecise, I still find the term androcentric (first coined by Kari Elisabeth Børresen, in *Subordination et equivalence: Nature et role de la femme d'apres Augustin et Thomas d'Aquin* [Oslo: Universitetsforlaget 1968], 8–9) useful

the struggle to overcome the oppression of women and the subordination of women to men; it is nurtured by a vision of justice and equality;
and for many it is rooted in the faith that God redeems and trans-
forms. It entails a critical examination of ideologically infected claims,
inherited prejudices, established discourses, and other structures of
power that have maintained woman as the second sex.

Feminist criticism is not a singular, monolithic position but a label
that covers a variety of approaches or methodologies, entering into
alliances with historical–critical methods, social-scientific criticism,
literary or narrative criticism, reader-response criticism, and, more
recently, postcolonial criticism. Strictly speaking, feminist criticism is
not a particular method of interpretation so much as it is a critical
sensibility, the application of a perspective emerging out of liberation
hermeneutics and contextual readings.

Feminist criticism calls for a scrutiny of Scripture by means of
reading strategies that do not evade the more or less explicit misogyny
of biblical texts but also help overrule this misogyny in creative and
liberating ways. It continues to confront a mainstream scholarship
that hesitates to recognize its vested male-stream interest and remains
enshrined in historical and related criticisms that regard themselves
as scientifically objective. Therefore, feminist criticism tends often to
distrust objective truth claims and to regard interpretations that claim
completeness and supremacy over all other readings as themselves
enactments of dominion. However, the assertion that the multivalence
of a biblical text allows different performances, hearings, and readings
should not lead to the conclusion that all are of equal value. Especially
from a liberation perspective, the hermeneutical privilege lies with of
the oppressed.

At the same time, there is in feminist criticism a professional
wrestling with the text that also serves as a protection against ideologically predictable results. Feminist criticism does not require that

and tend to prefer it to Luce Iragaray's more graphic term phallogocentrism, even
if the latter is more focused on the absence of woman/presence of man and what
women do not/cannot have (*Sexes and Genealogies* [New York: Columbia University
Press, 1993]).

scientific rigor is left behind. While drawing from the well of women studies and critical theory, feminist criticism most often also includes the specialized tools of biblical scholarship. As Adele Reinhartz wrote some years ago, "I do not hesitate to draw on the range of historical–critical method while acknowledging that the basic facts of my identity, as well as many other factors that may or may not be visible to me, will shape the exegetical process and its results, just as they have for all readers of this text."[6] Others might choose narrative or rhetorical analysis – the point still being that feminist criticism is not a method in itself but a critical perspective applying a variety of methods. This further involves that feminist critics may work independently of otherwise mutually exclusive positions on how meaning is constituted – that is, whether the text has a particular voice or embedded meaning of its own, which can be heard only if the interpreter suppresses his or her own voice; or whether the text is itself mute, capable of meaning only when a reader or interpreter makes sense of it. Interpreting from different social locations may also bring to light different aspects of a text, particularly when a text is seen to harbor a surplus of meaning or rather the potential of multivalence.

Reinhartz also warns that a confrontational – in her language "apocalyptic" – model of feminist criticism is undermined by its own reductionism because it does not do justice to the complexity of the larger situation. Efforts to be correct about gender may inscribe mistakes such as anti-Judaism when patriarchal features of Christianity are assigned to Judaism, relegating Judaism to serve as the scapegoat or dark backdrop against which the light of Christianity is thrown into sharp relief.[7] In the early phase of Christian feminist criticism, assumptions were often made about Judaism that might seem flattering to early Christianity but failed to recognize that early Judaism involved a similar variation of possible positions and, indeed, that

---

6 Adele Reinhartz, "Feminist Criticism and Biblical Studies on the Verge of the Twenty-First Century," in *A Feminist Companion to Reading the Bible: Approaches, Methods and Strategies* (ed. Athala Brenner and Carole Fontaine; Sheffield: Sheffield Academic Press, 1997), 30–8 (35).
7 Reinhartz, "Feminist Criticism," 33.

Jesus was himself a Jew, however radical or countercultural. In the particular case of Luke, there is good reason to believe that the Gospel was written in an environment deeply rooted in Hellenistic Judaism.

Feminist criticism comprises not only a methodological adaptability but also a plurality of theological positions. Women do not necessarily agree among themselves any more than men do, and today most feminists stand back from speaking of an overruling or essential "woman's experience" in which women share independently of other differences. Increasingly, feminist criticism has sought to express itself contextually, not promoting or depending upon a particular understanding or stereotype of what it is to be female or of "female experience." Rather, it should contribute to the liberation of women also from such stereotypes. A feminist approach is fundamentally a critical approach that unveils gender blindness and challenges traditions and positions that place "man" as a self-identical and ahistorical agent, who represents universality and normativity, and whose perspective consequentially is privileged and subsumes all others. All the more important is it that feminist criticism does not give in to the temptation to match this kind of universal discourse and speak oppositionally about "woman" in general.

GENDER AS ANALYTICAL CATEGORY

The introduction of gender as an analytical category has proven useful in exposing gender blindness.[8] It has helped to demonstrate how gender has an almost all-embracing structural significance; gender seems to be omnipresent and deeply embedded in the formation of the way in which we look at most things.[9] Gender is bodily inscribed but

---

[8] Joan W. Scott, "Gender: A Useful Category of Historical Analysis," *American Historical Review* 91 (1986): 1053–75. In "The Evidence of Experience," *Critical Inquiry* 17 (1991): 773–97, Scott develops this further to say that because the physical difference between men and women has no inherent meaning, one should explore how categories such as gender, class, race, and agency received their foundational status. Processes of signification stand prior to meaning and experience.

[9] Deborah Cameron, *The Feminist Critique of Language: A Reader* (London: Routledge, 1990), 1–28.

the significance attached to sexual attributes in determining gender may vary. Gender is not an unmarked category but articulated in forms of great variety in terms of culture and location in time and space. Poststructuralist gender studies have challenged the stability of the categories by which we characterize persons and strived to deconstruct the power structures that define "normality." Without necessarily accepting "queer theory," any investigation interested in gender has to take seriously that the terms "man" and "woman" cannot be used as if they were uniform and unified categories. Gender is not only a historically varied category; "it also does not affect all women in the same way or any women in the same way all the time."[10]

Studies focusing on the construction of masculinity have followed in the wake of feminist criticism and the heightened awareness about gender. Masculinity no longer retains "the invisibility of the norm" – which meant that women had to be mentioned to be present.[11] It is obvious that constructions of femininity/ies and masculinity/ies somehow are mutually dependent, and that how the mutual dependence and interplay between men and women are conceived should be investigated. It may be that portrayals of women in ancient texts say more about the construction of masculinity than about the actual lives of women.[12] However, within feminist criticism one should remain cautious and not accept too quickly a shift of focus from feminist criticism to studies of masculinity. Given the homosocial interest in the new male, the focus on masculinity may be another, more subtle way to marginalize women, another guise of seeing men as more important than women and paying attention to women primarily for how their presence in texts may contribute to the understanding of masculinity.[13]

[10]   Anonymous, "Feminist and Womanist Criticism," 237. See also in the following the section on "Intersectionality."
[11]   Mary Rose D'Angelo, "The ANER Question in Luke-Acts: Imperial Masculinity and the Deployment of Women in the Early Second Century," in *Feminist Companion to Luke*, 44–69 (44).
[12]   D'Angelo, "The ANER Question."
[13]   For these considerations, see Marianne Bjelland Kartzow, *Gossip and Gender: Othering of Speech in the Pastoral Epistles* (Acta Theologica 19; Oslo, 2007), 198–202.

HERMENEUTICAL SIGNPOSTS

The polarity of feminist positions on the Gospel of Luke exemplifies a more comprehensive pattern in the feminist interpretation of biblical texts. This pattern is also determined by the fact that feminist criticism has developed through several distinctive phases, each of which has left traces in its methodological repertory, resulting in a complex and diverse multitude of interpretive advances becoming operative simultaneously but yielding different and also conflicting results. One may distinguish among three main phases/approaches.[14]

The earliest studies that emerged during the resurgence of feminist biblical scholarship in the 1960s and 1970s tended to focus on the retrieval of unnoticed biblical texts about women. The aim was to uncover positive portrayals of women in the Bible and to focus upon feminine figures and symbols (images of women) in counterbalance to the masculine. This approach resulted in a multitude of often edifying compilations that helped affirm women in their femaleness by bringing forth biblical images of women as positive models of identification. It was and is multifaceted, but represents "a hermeneutics of recuperation."[15]

However, these early books on biblical women, still in vogue in some Christian circles, focus on the individual female figures subtracted from their wider context. The ideological force of discourse and the implications of a complex social matrix are not fully recognized. They rely on presuppositions of femininity as referential, assuming that somehow all women share in an essentially defined womanhood or women's experience. This is, however, not to say that they are unaware of the power structures that render women to silence and invisibility

---

[14] Cf. the popular but well-informed presentation by Emily Cheney, *She Can Read: Feminist Strategies for Biblical Narrative* (Valley Forge, Pa.: Trinity, 1996), 11; and Barbara Reid, *Choosing the Better Part? Women in the Gospel of Luke* (Collegeville, Minn.: Liturgical, 1996), 7–10. This presentation is not identical with either of these, but I have used them as a comprehensive starting point for further reflection. I also find the historical survey in *Postmodern Bible*, 244–87, informative, particularly its first part.

[15] *Postmodern Bible*, 245.

both in textual production and interpretation. Their quest assumes consciously a selective reading, subject to the partial view they are proud to represent. However, their project of retrieval still suffers from a lack of critical scrutiny and correction. They sweep the house as they look for the silver coin, and at times something glimmers in the dust. But they do not dare say that the state of the house itself is faulty.

A far more critical approach will simply leave the house behind, deeming it beyond repair and ready for condemnation. Misogyny is *Complete* seen as so pervasive that the Bible yields nothing but bitter fruit for *nonsense* women today. The biblical tradition is considered irredeemable for women even if some writings may be treated with more harshness than others. According to this view, the authority of Scripture in its traditional form is to be deconstructed and discounted and replaced by new, (re)constructed stories.

Also on a clearly critical note but less severe, some are not so much looking for images of women as for "golden rules" and a biblical message that continues to bring hope. In its outcome this quest is positive toward the biblical message, if not toward biblical texts. It employs a hermeneutics of liberation in that it discerns a certain strand or theme of biblical tradition, a prophetic-liberating message, and applies that as a criterion for evaluating particular texts. Taking struggle for justice as its point of departure it uses biblical authority toward its own justice-oriented ends.

Barbara Reid's work on women in the Gospel of Luke is an illuminating example of this latter approach, methodologically consistent and clear. Hers is a critical reading that sees the women not as protagonists but as victims. In the Lukan context, women are restricted by a patriarchal role division to supportive, silent roles. However, this confinement violates what Reid upholds as the liberating praxis of Jesus *G-g-* and his message, which makes Christianity redeemable. It becomes a case of Jesus against Luke. The voice and practice of Jesus are discerned by applying a hermeneutics of suspicion extracted from Luke's misleading contextualization and intent. Reid calls for a liberating recontextualization of the Lukan stories about women, negotiating new meaning through a deconstruction that sets the stories free to be reconstructed and reclaimed in ways usable to the church today. According to this view, Luke overrules the (historical) subtext of women's participation and leadership revealed by a hermeneutics of suspicion and comes close to a patriarchal reinforcement carried into prescriptive effect by the Pastoral Epistles.

The introduction of a hermeneutics of suspicion marks an important transition in feminist criticism.[16] A hermeneutics of suspicion is contrasted to a hermeneutics of consent and affirmation and represents an interpretative strategy of resistance where the authority of a biblical text lies in whether it helps end relations of domination and exploitation. It is ethical and theological in its focus and commitment. It also represents a change of perspective or relocation of the center and opens up to rhetorical and literary methods in order to bring forth the shadows and the silences – the victims – so that it may not happen again. As Phyllis Trible once stated with exemplary clarity: "By feminism I do not mean a narrow focus upon women, but rather a critique of culture in light of misogyny."[17]

By a radical shift of perspective, women are not just brought forth from the margins or depths of the often-forgotten stories. As they are moved to the center of the investigation, the understanding of the whole story is reconfigured. This lays bare the partialities and lacunae, all the cracks in the textual construction of early Christian history, and calls for a (feminist) reconstruction of Christian origins. A hermeneutics of suspicion is therefore only the first step in a further hermeneutical process leading to remembrance, reconstruction, and also proclamation whereby "the Scriptures offer paradigms for struggles and

---

[16]   This was introduced by Elisabeth Schüssler Fiorenza in several works in the 1980s – cf. *Bread Not Stone: The Challenge of Feminist Biblical Interpretation* (Boston: Beacon, 1984), 15. In *But She Said: Feminist Practices of Biblical Interpretation* (Boston: Beacon, 1992) this approach is further unfolded as a critical rhetorical process within the normative space of the *ekklesia* of women where biblical religions and cultures are being changed "in the interest of all women and marginalized people" (75–6).

[17]   Phyllis Trible, *God and the Rhetoric of Sexuality* (Philadelphia: Fortress, 1978), 7.

[handwritten: abandoning word for Spirit. Fejune,]

visions that are open to their own transformations through the power
of the Spirit in ever new socio-historical locations."[18]

In this approach, feminist interpretations are recontextualized readings where the context is defined by wider feminist reconstructions
of the earliest Christian movement or communities. This may be
achieved through a fairly conventional historical–critical analysis
including a conscious shift of perspective, but also through historically
informed imagination – that is, through playing with the possibilities
of what might have been.[19] In order to combat the massive process
that has rendered women invisible and silent, the critical project of
making women "heard and visible" should not be easily dismissed or
deemed to be an impossible mission because the sources are too fragile
or made impenetrable by their discursive confinement. It remains a
challenging task indeed, but it is a matter of solidarity through the
ages to recall the presence of women in the past and never cease to
explore whether their voices can be heard and their lives appreciated.

[handwritten margin note: Yes, why should a lack of evidence stop us?]

By means of a hermeneutics of remembrance that uses imaginative
intervention, women are written into history. This requires that traditional notions of historical significance are not only enlarged but
redefined. It goes beyond writing a new history of women. Rather, it
is instrumental in creating a new history – indeed, it changes history.
As Amy-Jill Levine states at the conclusion of her introduction to
A Feminist Companion to Luke: "What we recall when we look back
may be an evil that requires rejection, a repository of values that can
no longer be proclaimed, a tale of condemnation that masks another

---

[18] Schüssler Fiorenza, *But She Said*, 76.
[19] This is what Elisabeth Schüssler Fiorenza did in her groundbreaking book, *In Memory of Her: A Feminist Theological Reconstruction of Christian Origins* (New York:
Crossroad, 1983). Recently Carolyn Osiek and Margaret Y. MacDonald with Janet
M. Tulloch, *A Woman's Place: House Churches in Earliest Christianity* (Minneapolis,
Minn.: Fortress, 2006), have made a creative and knowledgeable attempt at exploring the social matrix and the material infrastructure in antiquity, and imagine how
women's life went on in a house that also served as church. They argue that "social
invisibility is conceptual; it exists in the minds of those who articulate the ideal and
may bear no resemblance to what is really going on." There is a move from text to
history as it may be socially reconstructed.

story . . . lost to recorded history. If we fail to remember, we too (like Lot's wife) will turn to stone; if we remain mired in the past rather than use what we remember to shape the future, we shall have failed the next generation."[20]

SUBJECTIVITY AND AGENCY

In a patriarchal system and/or androcentric consciousness, the potential of women's agency is regarded as threatening and uncontrollable. Hence, women are stripped of agency and displaced. The French poststructuralist Luce Iragaray goes as far as claiming that "woman has not yet taken place."[21] This means that women are characterized by absence and men by presence. Women exist only in relation to men as a mirror for male self-reflection in what she calls a phallogocentric construction of reality. In fact, in ancient Greek there was no generic term for woman; all terms applied to women were relational dependent on the various stages of life. Thus, according to Iragaray, the phallos and the logos collude or work symbolically together to maintain hegemonic male power. This is not a matter of blaming men; it is rather to describe a system where both men and women are made to regard maleness as the human norm. We do not know who woman is by herself, only who she is as "the other." This is very much the case in ancient texts. Women's presence is instrumental. They are not there on their own behalf but appear to illustrate a point or in reference to something else. The significance of women is secondary or referential. They are excluded from the power of defining the world. Women provide a tool with which male authors can "think" the values of their cultures. A woman in a text may simply stand for something else; she points to something else rather than herself serving as a symbol or an emblem.[22]

---

[20] *Feminist Companion*, 22.

[21] Iragaray, *Sexes and Genealogies*, 66. Jorunn Økland's work on 1 Cor 11 applies Iragaray's perspective in an intriguing manner (*Women in Their Place*).

[22] Elizabeth Clark, "The Lady Vanishes: Dilemmas of a Feminist Historian after the 'Linguistic Turn,'" *Church History* 67 (1998): 1–31 (25, quoting David Halperin).

Poststructuralist/postmodern positions such as this are illuminating but have led to a broadly accepted deconstruction of both subjectivity and agency. However, the historian Joan Scott has emphasized that poststructuralist theory does not deny that people act or that they have some control over their actions. Rather, it criticizes the liberal theory that assumes individuals are fully autonomous, self-creating actors. The issue is not agency per se, but the limits of the liberal theory of agency.[23] It is to my mind necessary to avoid a complete dispersal of identity and to hold on to some form of subjectivity and agency without affirming gender essentialism. Applying a hermeneutics of suspicion, the question could be why feminists should accept that "the decentering of the male subject eventually annihilated the female subject as well. Why were we told to abandon subjectivity just at the historical moment when women had begun to claim it?" "Why," Nancy Miller asks, "was the 'end of woman' authorized without consulting her?"[24] Instead, women should claim the right to name themselves, and not leave it to Adam. A basic assumption in many reconstructions where women are written into the history is therefore that women's abilities for agency do not disappear completely, even in oppressive systems. For the interpretation of Luke 21:1–4 that follows, this is a crucial observation.

THE MULTIVALENCE OF NARRATIVE

The Gospel of Luke, whatever genre it may be said to represent, is a narrative. Narrative texts have an inbuilt polyphony in that they allow for, and even may include, several contradictory voices. Narratives therefore lend themselves to serving as a testing ground for shifts of perspective. In the case of prescriptive texts such as letters or speeches, an audience (or rather a narrative framework or situation) may be elicited or deduced so that the author's voice is interpreted as part of a larger discussion. This kind of shadow-reading or looking for

---

[23] Joan Scott, "Women's History," in *New Perspectives on Historical Writing* (ed. Peter Burke; University Park: Pennsylvania State University Press, 1992), 42–66, 65–6.

[24] Cited in Clark, "The Lady Vanishes," 3.

counter-voices is nothing new in biblical scholarship. For most New Testament (NT) writings, a variety of possible adversaries or differing groups have been identified as lurking behind the text – holding other opinions or representing practices with which the author disagrees and which he seeks to correct. Traditionally, however, it has been the task of the interpreter to side with the author, and to bring the author's voice to force. The authority of the text is taken to be attached to and dependent upon the authority of the author's position.

For feminist criticism, as for other readings today, the issue of interpretative authority is more complex. Does it reside in the text, the reader, the community, or some combination of these? Brigitte Kahl has in her work on the Gospel of Luke developed a hermeneutics of conspiracy whereby a feminist counter-reading is inscribed right into the patriarchal text itself.[25] Drawing on her experience of patterns of communication in the former German Democratic Republic, Kahl explores how a text produced under either internal or external censorship reveals a self-contradictory narrative: What the words manifestly say masks coded propositions and hidden agendas. Obedient and subversive readers, opposing forces and positions condensed and brought together in a compromise formation, in textual splits and inconsistencies – these are blueprints of counter-reading that are all to be found in the text itself. Hence Kahl forcefully asks whether "the divergent interpretations of Luke indicate that the text in fact is inconsistent in the sense that it comprises extreme polarities in a 'compromise formation' created by a countercultural setting."[26]

This does not necessarily reflect a strategy conceived by a single author but may express real conflicts and struggles. In the case of Luke, the hermeneutics of conspiracy provides one lens by which to understand how Luke's two-volume work gives rise to divergent perspectives.

[25] Brigitte Kahl, "Reading Luke against Luke: Non-Uniformity of Text, Hermeneutics of Conspiracy and the 'Scriptural Principle' in Luke 1," in *Feminist Companion to Luke*, 70–88. The article begins with an acute diagnosis: "the relation between the authority of Scripture and the critique of Scripture remains as neuralgic a point in feminist and post-colonial hermeneutical debates as ever before. Who criticizes whom?"

[26] Kahl, "Reading Luke," 74.

Kahl assigns to Luke "a Janus-headedness" – which is to say that the stories Luke tells are "simultaneously a testimony to a liberating history of women and to its suppression by (love) patriarchalism."[27] Methodologically, Kahl states that rather than assuming too quickly or too simply a unity of the text – either negatively or positively – one should explore how this heterogeneity works. The question to be addressed is not only that the text is composed of diverse elements, but also upon which oppositions Luke's positions are built, and what significance the narrative arrangement renders to these voices of self-contradiction.[28]

My own feminist and narrative reading of Luke has an emphasis on ambiguity not dissimilar from the one identified by Brigitte Kahl.[29] What I have labelled "the double message" involves a double connotation in that it refers partly to a compositional device in Luke-Acts whereby parallel gender structures emerge, and partly to a striking ambiguity in this Gospel's positioning of women. Where we would prefer certitude and clarity about the role of women – whether prominent or marginal – the Lukan text seems to confuse the question by marginalizing women who have been given prominence in the story. The challenge is whether this can be explained in a meaningful way without distorting the textual evidence in one direction only or giving in to wishful thinking.

DIVERSITY, COMPLEXITY, AND INTERSECTIONALITY

When Elisabeth Schüssler Fiorenza suggested that the terms "kyriarchal" and "kyriocentric" should replace patriarchal and androcentric, her point was to underscore that domination is not simply a matter of patriarchal, gender-based dualism but of a more comprehensive, interlocking, hierarchically ordered structure of domination as evidenced in a variety of oppressions, such as racism, social deprivation, heterosexism, and colonialism.

---

[27] Kahl, "Reading Luke," 86.
[28] Kahl, "Reading Luke," 86.
[29] Seim, *Double Message*; see the Concluding Summary, 249–60.

The concept of intersectionality has tentatively been introduced into gender studies to consider the interdependence of multiple aspects of identity and to help address how various structures involving power influence and constitute each other in complex and changeable patterns. Intersectionality represents an attempt not only to list the various factors but to consider systematically how categories such as gender, sexual orientation, class, race, ethnicity, nationality, age, religion, and social location intersect. These factors cannot be understood separately as they both modify and reinforce each other. The term "intersectionality" goes back to Kimberlé Crenshaw and was used to translate black feminist thought to express how various cultural and social patterns of oppression and inequality are bound together.[30] As the theory was further developed, the applicability was extended to all women in order to understand how dichotomies or intersections of social inequality form a matrix of domination.[31]

How do factors such as gender, class, race, ethnicity, nationality, age, and religious affiliation interact and mutually inform each other? Within feminist studies the development of different branches such as womanist theology shows that the category "woman" cannot be used to erroneously homogenize the experiences of women but should take into account other important sources of variation that cut across it in important and complex ways. Categories leak. Race is gendered and gender is racialized. Different from queer theory, which emphasizes the deconstruction or destabilization of analytical categories and

---

[30] Multiracial feminist theory has played a crucial role in the development of intersectional critique. In Kimberlé Crenshaw, ed., *Critical Race Theory: The Key Writings That Formed the Movement* (New York: New Press, 1995), the African-American critique of white feminism's hegemony and exclusive practice is given a strong voice. See also Wendy Single-Rushton, "Looking for Difference?" in *Complexity: Interdisciplinary Communications 2006/2007* (ed. Willy Østreng; Oslo: Centre for Advanced Study at The Norwegian Academy of Science and Letters, 2008), 93–5.

[31] Especially by the sociologist Patricia Hill Collins, "Gender, Black Feminism, and Black Political Economy," *Annals of the American Academy of Political and Social Science* 586 (2000): 41–53. Cf. also S. A. Mann and D. J. Huffmann, "The Decentering of Second Wave Feminism and the Rise of the Third Wave," *Science and Society* 69 (2005): 56–91.

argues against fixed categories as simplifying social fictions, intersectionality motivates intra- and intercategorical approaches.

Sharon Ringe involves more explicitly a personal dimension when she describes how a feminist reading entails perspective, experience, and commitment all shaped by "the data of one's existence" such as gender, race, class, ethnicity, physical condition, and relationships in which one is involved, as they are transformed into experience. The data of social location intersect with events of personal, local, and global history, shaping a "commitment to the physical, psychological, and social well-being of all women."[32]

Such awareness of how various power structures intermingle, that is, how they mutually influence and constitute each other, is important to feminist criticism. However, the interaction may make it difficult to discern the category that at any time is the decisive factor when a person or a group is mistreated or discriminated against. Is Luke's interest in women, be it positive or negative, related to his broader concern for the poor and other marginalized groups? Or is it a sign of his emphasis on the success the Christian proclamation had in noble and well-off circles, because many of the women appear to be relatively wealthy? Does it ultimately matter which factor proves decisive in a particular situation because it never appears in splendid isolation?

READING LUKE

The Gospel of Luke features women in greater number than any other NT writing, including the Acts of the Apostles. As many as forty-two passages are concerned with women or with motifs that might be labeled as female – which is more than the other Gospels, even when taking into account their length. Most of these passages belong to the material special to Luke, which means that it is unique. Within this material, three-eighths of the total number of persons mentioned are women, whereas they comprise two-fifths of all named persons.

---

[32] Sharon H. Ringe, "An Approach to a Critical, Feminist, Theological Reading of the Bible," in *A Feminist Companion to Reading the Bible*, 159–63 (156).

Many of these Lukan stories about women have been important to Christian women in their reading of the Bible as they show women in the company of Jesus. One may wonder whether the heat of the feminist argument over Luke may partly reflect the fact that there is enough material to nurture a fire.

Another factor that has been extremely influential is the rarity that the Gospel of Luke is followed by a second volume, the Acts of the Apostles, most probably written by the same author, even if a second volume may not have been projected when the Gospel was written. In the second volume, which presupposes the Gospel, material on women is relatively scarce – or rather the appearance of women rises only to a level that is average when compared with the other narrative writings of the NT. The difference between the two volumes corresponds to the divergence in the perception regarding the treatment of women by Luke as it was presented previously. Which is most Lukan? Some feminist commentators seem to think that Luke finally got his say in Acts, having struggled in the Gospel with damage limitation, because the available traditions about Jesus had a stronger profile favoring women than what Luke himself approved of. It has, in other words, to quite some degree been a discussion of Luke's alleged fixed opinion or position. However, the project should not be to portray Luke's view of women, or to see women or gender as one theme among others in the Lukan texture. Then gender loses its force as an analytical category, and it is still an extremely author-oriented reading, assembling the meaning of a text as first and foremost a reflection of the author's mind and strategy. It is also an inadequate approach to the polyphony of a narrative and its potential for letting the reader in for accessing and assessing the story.

It is fair to say, providentially, that new and more complex ways of reading Luke with feminist eyes are now in place. In the introduction to *The Feminist Companion* quoted in the beginning to show contradictory approaches to women in the Gospel of Luke, we also read, "Rather than restrict explications of Luke's narrative to the artificial and reified dichotomies of good or bad news concerning gender roles, sexuality, emancipation, or any of the other categories that concern feminist analysis, commentators are increasingly recognizing the multiple messages as well as the partiality – in the dual sense of being both biased and incomplete – of each reading."[33]

Considering the fact that the Gospel of Luke is not a systematic treatise but a narrative opens up possibilities of polyphony and ambiguities. It tells a story, presents a sequence of events that form development or plot, in which the individual episodes take place at a particular stage in the larger, overarching narrative. The order is rarely arbitrary, and the location of various episodes in a narrative sequence can itself be an effective means of dealing with tensions and also with contradictions. A narrative is not a stable system; what we have is a complex movement. The narrative form invites polyphony and also discord. It allows for several and even contradicting voices to be heard in the course of the narrative. It may convey mixed or double messages, heterogeneity, without collapsing.

If the story moves from presence to absence, it may provide insight into mechanisms and structures of oppression and silencing. This balancing duality means that an analysis of the Gospel of Luke reveals conflict and debate, silencing structures and subversive survival.

LUKE 21:1–4: THE STORY OF THE WIDOW'S MITES

As Jesus looked up, he saw rich people throwing their gifts into the temple treasury; he also saw a certain poor widow throwing in two small copper coins, and he said, "Truly I tell you, this poor widow has put in more than all of them; for all these put in their gifts out of their abundance, but she has contributed out of her poverty everything she had to live on." (Luke 21:1–4)

This story or brief episode is common to the Gospel of Luke and the Gospel of Mark, and the two agree with regard to its location both

---

[33] *Feminist Companion to Luke*, 2.

topographically and narratively in that in both Gospels it follows upon a saying of Jesus in which he denounces the scribes:

"Beware of the scribes, who like to walk around in long robes, and love to be greeted with respect in the marketplaces, and to have the best seats in the synagogues and places of honor at banquets. They devour widows' houses and for the sake of appearance say long prayers. They will receive the greater condemnation." (Luke 20:46–47)

A Feminist Look at Current Interpretations

Most commentators pay little attention to the brief episode, and there are also remarkably few individual contributions elucidating it. This situation may be due to a convenient consensus as to the purpose and meaning of the story. In a much-read commentary, this consensus is briefly stated in the following manner:

These words of Jesus express the deepest convictions of the Christian community concerning its understanding of the kingdom of God. God owns all things and all things must be given back to God. This allegiance transcends every political expression.

The kingdom shaped by such a Lord is entirely new with the newness of God's own life: it is neither the perpetuation of a national dream of sovereignty nor can it be portrayed in terms of earthly preoccupations about descent and property. This kingdom is symbolized by the widow, who though left alone in human terms, is not herself alive but capable of giving life by sharing all her living with others.[34]

This latter point may be further developed to serve as an image of the scandal of the cross, in that the widow who gives her whole life prefigures Jesus' own submission of his very life on behalf of others.[35] On the whole, in this interpretation the woman in the story serves a

---

[34] Luke Timothy Johnson, *The Gospel of Luke* (SP 3; Collegeville, Minn.: Liturgical, 1991), 318–19.

[35] Elizabeth Struthers Malbon, "The Poor Widow in Mark and Her Poor Rich Readers," *CBQ* 53 (1991): 589–604. Even if the article deals with the Markan account, interpreters tend to treat the episode as a synoptic story without differentiating between the versions.

symbolic or emblematic purpose; she provides a tool with which the author and also interpreters can "think," symbolizing the kingdom and/or prefiguring Jesus' own sacrificial submission in death.

The remarkable reserve among commentators when it comes to dealing with this story is, however, not sufficiently explained either by a convenient consensus or by its meagre brevity. More likely, it is due to the fact that the story is felt to be, at best, ethically ambiguous and certainly not politically correct to socially conscientious minds today. Most commentators remain troubled by the idea that Jesus would (re)commend, not to say laud, a poor widow who gave up to the temple what little she had.

In 1982, Addison G. Wright offered another, radically different inter-pretation that has come to represent the attractive alternative to the established consensus, which with minor differences assumes that the poor widow should be revered as an exemplary character or symbol.[36] According to Wright, the story serves as a lament and as an exemplifi-cation of the preceding verse where Jesus condemns the mighty scribes for their vain hypocrisy and exploitation of widows. Hence it does not praise the woman's generosity. It is rather a complaint and an accusa-tion against those who have led her astray by false pretensions of piety. Jesus first attacks the scribes for their economic encroachments upon widows. The narrative or rather the observation that follows in 21:1–4 is a condemnation of the temple authorities, who, like the scribes, deprive a widow of her living – although admittedly in a more subtle way. Jesus laments the system that takes advantage of widows such as her. The poor widow is a victim to the instruction by the religious leaders who have misdirected her to support her own oppression.

This recasting of the episode has for obvious reasons had a great following.[37] It makes sense of the story's textual location in that it establishes a narrative continuity both with what precedes it and with the apocalyptic discourse about the destruction of the temple that

---

[36] Addison G. Wright, "The Widow's Mites: Praise or Lament? A Matter of Context," *CBQ* 44 (1982): 256–65.

[37] Also by Joseph Fitzmyer in his influential Anchor Bible Commentary, *The Gospel According to Luke* (2 vols.; Garden City, N.Y.: Doubleday, 1985), 2: 1319–22.

follows. Even more importantly, it solves the ethical dilemma and puts right and wrong back in place: the poor should be protected and defended, not falsely encouraged to give up what little they have.[38] The poor widow is no longer to be regarded as an illustrious example or symbol of great values. She should be bewailed as a victim of false and vain pretenders who dress up exploitation in the guise of piety. She is, according to Stephen Moore, "epitomizing the oppressed peasantry mercilessly bled dry by the indigenous, Rome-allied elites." Indeed, it is because of "what has been done to the weakest of the weak in its name that the Jerusalem temple has been marked by God for demolition."[39] The two copper coins, which represented her livelihood, were far too small an amount to make a difference to the income of the temple. Furthermore, in the verses immediately following the poor widow's action, the destruction of the temple is predicted – which is to say that her gift to a place where not one stone will be left upon another is simply wasted. The widow's sacrifice is thus not only tragically misdirected; the pending destruction of the temple serves to intensify the futility of the widow's sacrifice of her livelihood. It would indeed be absurd if not for the possibility that it is less about the poor widow than about Jesus himself, and his giving and dying.[40]

The exegetical rescue operation on the poor widow's behalf also happens at a cost – at her cost. She is consistently construed as an object, intersectionally accumulating in her person the double misery of poverty and widowhood. We are not even allowed to hear the victim's scream in her, but rather are left to observe how oppressive power systems silently seduce by making people act against their own interests. Thus, in the story she is exposed to the exploitation of the rich and mighty Jerusalem elite, and in the interpretation she becomes the object of the compassionate and patronizing concern of the interpreter. Either way, the dignity of being regarded as an agent in her own

---

[38] This is, of course, not a laughing matter, and if Barbara Reid is right in saying that contemporary Christian development campaigns often appeal to her as the model donor (*Choosing the Better Part?*, 195), this comes close to yet another form of exploitation.

[39] Stephen Moore, *Empire and Apocalypse: Postcolonialism and the New Testament* (Sheffield: Phoenix, 2006), 41–3.

[40] Malbon, "Poor Widow."

right is not acknowledged. She is denied any responsibility of her own as her identity and role are exhausted in the delusion imposed on her. She is simply another victim, subject only to pity and compassion – except, of course, for her emblematic value.

In her interpretation of the story of the widow's mites, Barbara Reid ends up claiming the openness of a reader-response criticism and thus accumulating these various interpretations. The story has no particular true meaning. It is open-ended – conveying a different meaning depending on where one stands.[41] For those who would align themselves with the voracious scribes, it offers a challenge to reject all ways of feeding off of the poorest, particularly under the guise of religion. For those who are oppressed and poor, it issues an invitation to reject giving support to those very systems that treat them unjustly. Finally, the action of the widow is a foretaste of Jesus, offering of his entire life, an offering made from his position of poverty and not of wealth. However, these three options return the feminist reader to the traditional options of either lamenting another case of a woman being the victim or praising the self-sacrifice that represents the ultimate virtue and brings redemption. Even if many readings are possible, does everything depend on the reader?

Stephen Moore is sensitive enough to see the problem of victimizing the widow and offers as a possibility a third reading that "piggy-backs on the traditional ecclesiastical reading" and moves in the direction of styling the widow as an exemplary figure, not because she anticipates Jesus' own self-emptying in death, but rather because she exceeds it: "The woman's voluntary self-divestment of 'everything she had, all she had to live on' – at once an absolute and thankless gesture – may be read as an act of epiphanic extravagance whose immeasurable immoderation thrusts it outside every conventional circle of economic exchange."[42] In applying to the widow's offering Jacques Derrida's concept of a gift beyond reciprocity, her self-divestment becomes an expenditure without reserve and an absolute gift. It represents "the breaking through, or breaking out of something inconceivable, hardly

---

[41] Reid, *Choosing the Better Part?*, 197.
[42] Moore, *Empire and Apocalypse*, 42.

possible, *the* impossible, even."[43] Moore's third way may be void of christological implications but apart from the Derridarian discourse, which softens the moral blow by its cushion of boundary-breaking claims to excessiveness and anomality, it does indeed ride on the back of the old consensus interpretation.[44]

Moving the Woman to the Center

The following is an attempt at moving the woman to the center of the Lukan story, focusing upon the characterization of her and the connotations this evokes in a contextual perspective. It accepts that in the story of the widow's mites, as is often the case, we learn nothing about the feelings, reflections, and attitude on the part of the woman, and that it may be intrusive to claim what those might be. The silence and restrictions of the text should be respected. Even in its more imaginative versions, feminist criticism does not necessarily entail that the woman should come alive as a fully embodied person – even if some are tempted to fill in the silences of the text in order to make the widow meet the modern reader's need for a full-fledged portrayal, presenting the reasons for her action and how she might possibly feel about it. What we are told is that this woman is a widow and that she is poor.

The Woman Is a Widow

It is important to read the Lukan version of the story in view of its specific features in relation to Mark as well as the wider Lukan context. Whereas a widow is a rarity in Mark, in Luke-Acts, widows appear more often than in any other NT writing. In the Lukan context, any passage where a widow appears becomes part of the wider discourse

---

[43] Moore, *Empire and Apocalypse*, 43.

[44] Moore writes primarily with a view to the context of the Gospel of Mark, and in this attempt at "a third reading" he finds an indication of "liminal experiments in a community that apocalyptically deconstruct the world as we know it." Indeed, the anecdote of the Widow's Mites may be "the real site of apocalypse in Mark," and accordingly it may "render the apocalyptic metanarrative superfluous and hence expendable." Whereas Moore's interpretation of the episode might possibly apply also to the Lukan version, the immediate contextualization would have to be different.

on widows involving four major narratives and examples unique to the Gospel of Luke in which widows are explicitly mentioned: the prophetess Anna (2:36–38), the widow at Sarephath (4:25–26), the widow at Nain (7:11–17), and the importunate widow (18:1–8).[45] Moreover, it has been suggested that most of the other women who in this Gospel narrative appear independently and "without a husband" might be widows. This applies to Peter's mother-in-law (4:38–39) and to Martha (10:38–42).[46] However, apart from Anna, the term widow is not applied to any named women.

In ancient texts, widows appear to be ambiguous characters. On the one hand the widow – sometimes together with the orphan – may serve as the epitome of need – short of support and not able to fend for herself. Etymologically the term χήρα (*chēra*) means "someone left without a lord/man." It is characteristic that the masculine form of the noun is much newer and was hardly ever used.[47] On the other hand, a widowed woman had greater freedom than she ever had as a young girl or as a wife. She had the right to be consulted in questions that concerned her own life and was allowed to decide for herself in matrimonial matters. Especially in a Roman context, the *univira* was an ideal, that is, a young widow who remained chaste after her husband's death, faithful to her deceased husband for the rest of her life.[48] Judaism was also acquainted with a pietism for which widows served as models. Judith, who remained a widow after the death of her husband Mannaseh and lived a life marked by chastity and fasting (Jdt 8:6), was such an ideal figure in the pious imagination of the Maccabean period. The prophet Anna in Luke 2:36–38 is clearly designed in similar terms.

The figure of a widow therefore carries an ambivalent connotation of exceptional need and exceptional freedom of agency. Most of the

---

[45] One might also mention the widows of the Hellenists in Acts 6:1 and the widows in Tabitha's house in Acts 9:36–42. These are both important when it comes to establishing a possible social framework within which the Lukan interest in widows might be situated.

[46] In Acts, Mary the mother of John (12:12) and Lydia (Acts 16:14–40).

[47] For this and the following, cf. Seim, *Double Message*, 229–48.

[48] In Christian tradition, this may have contributed to a convergence between widows and virgins (Ign. *Smyrn.* 13.1).

Lukan narratives about widows exploit this ambivalence.[49] Apart from the miracle stories, widows are portrayed as vulnerable; however, they are not cast as recipients but as persons of perseverance.

The exposed, vulnerable position of the widow is combined with an emphasis on strength and piety. Luke 21:1–4 cannot be read without listening to the echo of this ambivalence.

The Widow Is Poor

In this story about the widow's mites, the Gospel of Luke follows Mark in accentuating that the widow is poor. It is not possible to make very much of the distinction between χήρα πτωχή (*chēra ptōchē*, "poor widow") in Mark and χήρα πενιχρά (*chēra penichra*, "poor widow") in Luke, because Luke immediately afterward calls her πτωχή (*ptōchē*, "poor"). Nevertheless, the repeated emphasis on the poverty of this widow increases the contrast with the rich and gives her example all the more strength.

The episode as told in the Gospel of Luke marks the difference between the widow and the rich with considerably greater sharpness than the Gospel of Mark. In the Lukan version, Mark's crowd is conspicuous by its absence, and the focus is exclusively on the rich. Nor does the Gospel of Luke follow Mark in saying that the rich gave much. These variations between Luke and Mark are hardly ever taken to be of much significance, and the two versions are treated as if they say the same thing.[50] However, the Lukan version establishes a sharper contrast by limiting the comparison within the episode itself to two clear-cut parties, one rich and the other poor. In Luke, as in Mark,

---

[49] Cf. the suggestion that the women who have their own households might be widows, which is all the more remarkable because it is often assumed that Luke's interest in widows belongs to "his broader interest in the oppressed and despised, especially the poor and women" (G. Stählin, "χήρα," *TDNT* 9: 440–65 [450]). See also Bonnie Bowman Thurston, *The Widows: A Women's Ministry in the Early Church* (Minneapolis, Minn.: Fortress, 1989), 25.

[50] For example, in his influential article, Wright explicitly states that his "remarks are seen as valid for the story both in Mark and in Luke. The context in both gospels is identical and the difference in wording between the versions is minor" ("The Widow's Mites," 263).

the poor widow constitutes also another contrast – to the snobbish greed of the scribes against which Jesus warns in the previous saying in 20:45–47. The scribes devour the houses of widows and pretend to pray. If the two accusations are connected with each other, which is likely, then the latter is far more than an accusation of hypocrisy. The scribes are condemned because they extort from widows under the pretext of performing long and well-paid prayers for them. Given the fact that widows in other Lukan passages are portrayed as models of persevering prayer, the accusation assumes a strong note of irony. The irony is further reinforced as the poor widow, victim of their mismanagement, is presented immediately afterward as the one who displays true piety.

The contrast and the effect of irony are lost to those who follow Wright's argument and do not see beyond the widow's misery as a victim. They simply make the connection to the preceding verses and limit the perspective so that the widow just becomes a further exemplification of the scribes' encroachment on widows. However, the alleged victim is rather the protagonist whose act should be emulated and not lamented. This is also made clear by Jesus' words of praise. However, it is significant that Jesus does not speak to the widow and that her action precedes his words.[51] The addressees are his disciples, probably still "in the hearing of all the people" (20:45), as he comments on what they have all seen her do at her own initiative.

The Poor Widow's Agency

In relation to the disciples, the poor widow's action is doubly paradigmatic in that it states an example as well as issues a warning. Positively, and to my mind there is no way around this in the context of Luke-Acts, the poor widow's deed is exemplary in that she gives the little she has to support her life. Her action must be seen in light of the ideal of giving up one's property and even one's life in passages such as

---

[51] This is one of the reasons why the episode of the widow's mites by some interpreters is taken to function almost as a parable.

12:22–34, which voice a general ideal of abandonment, of not investing in material future security. Even if this interpretation may seem to move in the direction of having the woman making sense primarily by what she signifies, she is not reduced to serving as an illustration of something else. She is still an agent, and her agency is recognized as praiseworthy.[52]

The widow's action is also a caution: Jesus warns his followers to guard against acting like the scribes. The deficiency of those in power is exposed by the poor widow's action. Hence, the passage of the poor widow's mites serves in the Gospel of Luke as a severe instance of leadership criticism. Indeed, in this Gospel there are two stories where the current leadership is confronted by a critical corrective represented by a woman's action. It first happens during the Galilean period in Luke 7:36–50, where a prostitute gatecrashes a party where Jesus is a guest, and the Pharisee host is – according to Jesus – critically exposed by a woman's self-determined action. "Do you see this woman?" Jesus asks the Pharisee Simon in Luke 7:44.[53]

In Luke's narrative the Pharisees appear as the main adversaries outside of Jerusalem. While Jesus is in Jerusalem, where the story about the widow's mites is located, other groups are the predominant antagonists, namely, the scribes, the temple hierarchy, and the rich nonpriestly aristocracy.[54] The story of the widow's mites might

---

[52] Even if the discourse is different and to my mind problematic, Bonnie Thurston probably intends something similar in her version of the former consensus interpretation: "in the ministry and teaching of Jesus, the widow appears as one of many examples of a new system of values breaking into the world. The widow's position and piety are no more to be lamented; she becomes exemplary. She is elevated to a position of spiritual prominence in the Christian order of things" (*Widows*, 27). Even closer is Stephen Moore, who in the end acknowledges that the poor widow's action of abandonment shows that she courageously and drastically trusts in God alone. Without a man to support her and without property, she lives a life with a radical eschatological orientation (*Empire and Apocalypse*, 43).

[53] For further elaboration, cf. Seim, *Double Message*, 88–95.

[54] Halvor Moxnes, *The Economy of the Kingdom: Social Conflict and Economic Relations in Luke's Gospel* (Minneapolis, Minn.: Fortress, 1988), 68–70. In Jerusalem, "Luke's focus is again upon Jesus' conflict with the elite, the leaders, while the people, here the 'urban nonelite,' stand at the side and are largely undifferentiated. . . . [I]ndividuals are only singled out when they are needed for the narrative of Jesus, as representatives of the ordinary, 'small' people of the city (19:33; 21:1–4;

therefore, despite all differences, be seen as a pendant to the story in Luke 7:36–50 in relation to the exposure of the Jerusalem elite that her action represents.[55] In contrasting comparison with the rich – who, seen from the perspective of quantity, give more than her but, relatively speaking, actually offer less – the widow acts in an exemplary manner. Do you see this widow? By making such a radical act of abandonment, she exposes their act as hypocritical and as lacking the dimension of self-sacrificing generosity. They pretend to be what their acts betray.

Jesus' words in 21:2–4 are probably still addressed to the direct and indirect audience constituted to hear his denouncement of the scribes in 20:45: "In the hearing of all the people he said to his disciples. . . . " The leadership it deplores is named but not directly addressed. The leadership is blamed in the face of those whom they should serve, and portrayed as antitypes to the ideals of management represented by Jesus himself and his disciples. As the Gospel of Luke antitypically describes this, it renders an exemplary significance to the action of women – positively in relation to the people of God and its new leadership, and negatively in relation to its present leadership.

It is possible to discern in the Gospel of Luke a terminological transfer of *diakon*-terms (διακον-, "to serve") from being attached exclusively to women, then to servants, before being spelled out in ideal terms with Jesus himself as an example for the new leaders of the people of God. They are told, according to Luke 22:26–27, to

22:10–13, 56; 23:39–43)" (68). Moxnes further observes, "In the first part of the passion narrative there is a concentration of references to money and economic interaction. First comes the expulsion of vendors from the temple (19:45–46); next, the question about tribute to Caesar (20:20–26); and finally, the widow's gift to the temple treasury (21:1–4). These instances are all related to the system of redistribution through a central authority. The authority that Jesus challenges in these narratives is the power to control the collection and redistribution of resources belonging to the Jewish people" (70).

55 However, the two stories do not constitute a pair. Regarding the Lukan tendency to generate doublets and *par alleles*, among them also "gender pairs," see Seim, *Double Message*, 11–24, and the comments and alternative interpretation by Mary Rose D'Angelo in "Women in the Gospel of Matthew and Luke-Acts," in *Women and Christian Origin* (ed. Ross S. Shephard and Mary Rose D'Angelo; New York: Oxford University Press, 1999), 181–4.

act "*as* one who serves."[56] It is not a pattern of a reversal of roles. Rather the leaders are to enter into functions of service that would not normally be indicated by their status. It is rather a matter of charging the role of leadership with an odd role model. What takes place is a corrective blending of two interdependent yet opposite roles or functions. Thereby in the sequence of the narrative, the actions of women are by way of Jesus' placing himself in the same role in 22:27, converted to an ideal to be followed by the new leadership of the people of God. This is, however, a leadership from which women are excluded, because maleness is stated as an explicit criterion for eligibility.[57] The idealization may seem to exalt them as model agents but it happens at their cost. If women's access to leadership positions is the litmus test by which their role and participation are judged, the Gospel of Luke ends up as a lost cause as the reader moves to Luke's second volume, the book of Acts. This has also been the case of the poor widow at the temple treasury.

However, more recently, I have become critical of the almost single-minded – though often highly sophisticated – interest among many feminist interpreters, including myself, in exploring the access or lack of access of women to (public) positions of leadership in early Christian communities and seeing this as the litmus test for the status and role of women. This interest primarily mirrors a search

---

[56] Luke 22:24–27 is one of the passages that is difficult to accommodate within the overall interpretation of John N. Collins, *Diakonia: Reinterpreting the Ancient Sources* (New York: Oxford University Press, 1990); he claims that "deacon" did not designate primarily the menial task of serving at table, which has been the common view dependent on H.W. Beyer's influential article, "διακονέω κτλ," *TDNT* 2: 81–93. It rather denotes a go-between in a range of activities. Whereas Collins helps us to understand better the usage of *diakon*-terms in the Pauline letters, the Gospels seem to reflect a further stage where a certain Christian usage has been established. I find Warren Carter's embrace of Collins in "Getting Martha out of the Kitchen: Luke 10.38–42," in *A Feminist Companion to Luke*, 214–31, unconvincing, especially because he exploits Collins further to eliminate "domestic or culinary activity" and claims that *diakonia* in Luke "indicates leadership and proclamation on behalf of God or the church and the gospel" (220–2).

[57] For a fuller discussion of this, see Seim, *Double Message*, 57–96, and the comments made by Veronica Koperski, "Women and Discipleship in Luke 10.38–42 and Acts 6.1–7: The Literary Context of Luke-Acts," in *A Feminist Companion to Luke*, 161–96.

for self-affirmation shaped by certain institutional constraints and for arguments supporting women's ambitions and aspirations in today's church and society. The search represents a legitimate struggle in which I wholeheartedly participate but when certain, and for feminists important, tasks (when we speak of equal opportunity) are not ascribed to women in the Gospel of Luke, this biblical text is deemed to fail us. Is this partly why Luke has become such contested ground? Do we not underestimate the hermeneutics of conspiracy or the dangerous remembrance subversibly hidden in texts such as this story in the Gospel of Luke?[58] Even when the women have been overruled, they continue to speak as their agency is recognized.

In the story of the poor widow at the temple treasury her action is the praiseworthy example whereby the Jerusalem elite is exposed to shame and disgrace. By giving up her life, she practices as well as exemplifies the radical requirements of discipleship, because survival is ultimately achieved by giving up one's present life in order to gain life immortal. This is the eschatological dimension retained also in the Gospel of Luke, converted into an ascetic ethos of abandonment and thereby both suspending and maintaining eschatological excitement.

Women in the Gospel of Luke are, like many men, not unexpectedly employed emblematically. Nevertheless, they are not entirely to be regarded or treated as stand-ins for virtues. There is an agency at work without which the exemplary significance would be void. Indeed, women's abilities for agency do not disappear completely – even in oppressive systems.

In an intriguing reading of the use of slavery in the hymn in Phil 2:6–11, Sheila Briggs develops an approach that observes how

understanding has an intuitive component which can acknowledge but not describe dimensions of reality that cannot be empirically known. Therefore we must reformulate the uses of analogy in historiography to take into account the hermeneutic intuition and its respect for the integrity of the past. The analogy becomes the comparison between the

---

[58] "The Gospel of Luke," in *Searching the Scriptures. A Feminist Commentary* (ed. Elisabeth Schüssler Fiorenza; New York: Crossroad, 1994), 728–63.

unknown of the present and the unknown of the past, between that which eludes the deployment of knowledge as a means of social control in the present and that which in the past resisted the hegemony of the symbolic universe, prescribed by the social elites.[59]

This analogy of the unknown of the present and the unknown of the past should heighten the contemporary reader's awareness that possible meanings, given to the texts by the oppressed, may be improbable or impossible meanings *in* the text. Applied to Phil 2:6–11, this means that the subjectivity that might have been the slaves as they subverted the text of Phil 2:6–11 is not historiographically recoverable. It is a past that can only be invented, a theological task proper to the narrative creativity of biblical proclamation within the communities of the oppressed today – assuming subjectivity by agency.

Althea Spencer Miller makes a similar move in her exposition of Luke 21:1–4 – including also the preceding verses in 20:46–47.[60] To some extent she builds on the interpretation that casts the poor widow as a victim of exploitation by the temple authorities. However, her reading persona, Lucy Bailey, opens up a space of resistance, and the article is "a libation to this ancestress in faith." Lucy Bailey was a Caribbean woman who died at the age of eighty, having earned her minimal livelihood as a household helper: "quite poor, quite under-educated, quite black, quite small in an age where each of these attributes was sub-status quo." But she excelled in lived learning and had always something to give.[61] Lucy Bailey firmly believed that she was counted among God's righteous, and in her community she used the words of the powerful to subvert their very power. Independently of whether she understood this or not, she possessed and she used subversive knowledge.

[59] Sheila Briggs, "Can an Enslaved God Liberate: Hermeneutical Reflections on Philippians 2:6–11," *Semeia* 47 (1989): 137–53 (141).
[60] Althea Spencer Miller, "Lucy Bailey Meets the Feminists," in *Feminist New Testament Studies: Global and Future Perspectives* (ed. Kathleen O'Brien Wicker, Althea Spencer Miller, and Musa W. Dube; New York: Palgrave MacMillan, 2005), 209–44.
[61] Miller, "Lucy Bailey," 209.

By learning from the experience of Lucy Bailey, and with Lucy Bailey as a lens for reading the story of the widow's mites, the widow, however poor and exploited, appears not simply and sadly as victimized. She exercises the might that is a product of her mites. She provides the criterion for judgment against the scribes. She displays "the column on which the pretentious base their ostentation." The point is that the emphasis is on her action and gift, not herself. Also Jesus had to look up to see her, but her might is her mites as the system would remain hidden without the widow and her offering – which is also her allegiance to the system that exploits her. Hers is the contrasting prism that clarifies the distortion, and with her very action she expresses the need of an ethic of prophetic justice. Indeed, a feminist counter-reading is found inscribed right into this patriarchal text itself.

The poor widow cannot be discounted; she is right there revealing the wisdom of subversive knowledge. This is no small change.

4

↓

Narrative Criticism

Joel B. Green

We refer to the wider discipline of studying the nature, form, and functioning of narrative texts as *narratology*,[1] but in biblical studies a constellation of interests and a variety of practices in the study of narrative have consolidated under the heading of *narrative criticism*. As a mode of study, narrative criticism would seem to require little by way of justification, because the first five books of the New Testament (NT), the Gospels and Acts, are each cast in narrative form, but lingering questions about the literary unity of these documents and the significant differences between ancient and contemporary narratives press for care in the construction of a narrative–critical method.

FROM THERE TO HERE: THE RISE OF NARRATIVE CRITICISM

With precedents far back in the history of interpretation, any time readers took seriously how the Bible tells stories and promoted the practice of close reading, narrative criticism in the modern era surfaced prominently in the 1980s. At the outset, narrative study was limited by its overly narrow focus on the texts themselves, as if texts could and ought to be regarded as self-sufficient, self-contained verbal artifacts. Accordingly, the text was presumed to be the unique and privileged source of meaning, with "meaning" available to the

---

[1] See Gerald Prince, *Dictionary of Narratology* (Lincoln: University of Nebraska Press, 1987), 65.

interpreter only by means of careful attention to its language and structure, without regard for concerns of a social–historical kind and with no sensible way to account for how or why different readers might understand the same narrative differently. As practiced in university departments of literature, however, *narratology* quickly engaged in self-correcting maneuvers that allowed narratology to move in multiple directions. Today, narratology increasingly blurs the lines between author, text, and reader. This, together with longstanding interests in historical questions and rapidly emerging concerns with readerly interests and social-scientific approaches to biblical texts, led many proponents and practitioners of *narrative criticism* in biblical studies to develop the discipline so as to account for how narratives are implicated in cultural criticism as well as how they engage – and are engaged by – their manifold readers.[2]

Published in 1981, Robert Alter's *The Art of Biblical Narrative* signaled what was then a radical call to enjoy the stories of the Bible

---

[2] Hence, Stephen D. Moore's criticism of literary study of the Gospels in the 1970s and 1980s for its overdependence on New Criticism was well aimed even if his pessimistic conclusions regarding the future potential of narrative study were premature (*Literary Criticism and the Gospels: The Theoretical Challenge* [New Haven, Conn.: Yale University Press, 1989]). Not all narrative critics are so willing to locate the study of NT narratives *vis-à-vis* historical analysis or, for that matter, in relation to readers. Mark Allan Powell's work is significant for the way it accounts for readerly interests. Although his study *What Is Narrative Criticism?* (GBS; Minneapolis, Minn.: Fortress, 1990) locates the text in its final form at center stage, his subsequent studies make transparent the role of the reader in actualizing narrative texts – for example, Mark Allan Powell, *Chasing the Eastern Star: Adventures in Biblical Reader-Response Criticism* (Louisville, Ky.: Westminster John Knox, 1991); idem, *What Do They Hear? Bridging the Gap between Pulpit and Pew* (Nashville, Tenn.: Abingdon, 2007). On the other hand, in what is currently the most recent handbook on narrative criticism, *Narrative Criticism of the New Testament: An Introduction* (Grand Rapids, Mich.: Baker Academic, 2005), James L. Resseguie maintains the sort of more restricted focus on the narrative-as-text that Moore aptly criticized. In a recent essay, Petri Merenlathi presses for narrative criticism to tackle the need for a more integrated hermeneutical reflection and reconsideration of the whole framework of biblical interpretation ("The Future of Narrative Criticism: A Paradigm Shift," in *Poetics for the Gospels? Rethinking Narrative Criticism* [SNTW; London: T. & T. Clark, 2002], 115–30). See also David Rhoads, "Narrative Criticism: Practices and Prospects," in *Characterization in the Gospels: Reconceiving Narrative Criticism* (ed. David Rhoads and Kari Syreeni; JSNTSup 184; Sheffield: Sheffield Academic Press, 1999), 264–85.

as stories by taking seriously those elements comprising the artistry of
biblical narrative.[3] Alter's focus was the Hebrew Bible, but the sorts
of questions he emphasized would be of interest to readers of NT
narratives as well. What are the roles of characters and characterization in biblical narrative? How are scenes composed? What is the
significance of repetition in the narrative texts of the Bible? What
does the narrator tell the reader and what information is withheld?
To a discipline occupied with sources and redaction, and otherwise
accustomed to reading narrative texts in the Bible not so much as continuous narratives but in piecemeal fashion, these were extraordinary
questions. A year later, David Rhoads and Donald Michie (one an NT
scholar, the other an English professor) opened up to readers the power
of the Gospel of Mark, understood as a narrative whole. "When we
enter the story world of the Gospel of Mark," reads their opening
line, "we enter a world full of conflict and suspense, a world of surprising reversals and strange ironies, a world of riddles and hidden
meanings."[4] The unity of the final text, the power of narrative to
shape its readers (or hearers), the construction of characters within
the Gospel as characters in a story, the compositional art of Mark's
narrative – with such emphases as these, Rhoads and Michie plunge
their readers of a quarter-century ago into a world of Gospels-study
for which they would have had little preparation.

Why would students of the Gospels and Acts be ill prepared for
reading the Gospels as stories?[5] On the one hand, those reared in
the church often have little exposure to the Gospel of Matthew or
the Acts of the Apostles as narrative wholes. The line, "Tell me the
stories of Jesus," may represent the interests of some congregations
and their programs of education, but it is rare for those stories – that

---

[3] Robert Alter, *The Art of Biblical Narrative* (New York: Basic, 1981).

[4] David Rhoads and Donald Michie, *Mark as Story: An Introduction to the Narrative
of a Gospel* (Philadelphia: Fortress, 1982), 1; see now David Rhoads, Joanna Dewey,
and Donald Michie, *Mark as Story: An Introduction to the Narrative of a Gospel*
(2nd ed.; Minneapolis, Minn.: Fortress, 1999).

[5] For what follows, I have drawn from Joel B. Green, "Narrative and New Testament
Interpretation: Reflections on the State of the Art," *Lexington Theological Quarterly*
39 (2004): 153–66.

is, those individual accounts of events in the life of Jesus – to be set interpretively within the larger narrative cotexts of the particular Gospel in which they appear. The Woman at the Well or Zacchaeus was a Wee Little Man take on a life of their own, quite apart from their Gospel settings. Nor has critical study of the Gospels and Acts provided much assistance. It is simply the case that the disciplined concerns of narrative criticism have appeared at the forefront of the study of the Gospels and Acts only in recent years. Let me illustrate briefly:

Augustine concluded that the Gospel of Mark was an abridgement of Matthew,[6] effectively relegating the Second Gospel to the margins. When, in the latter half of the eighteenth century, Mark was rediscovered, it surfaced primarily as a source book for the historical Jesus. In the early twentieth century, the Second Evangelist moved into the limelight of critical scrutiny, but his potential contribution as a narrator was brushed aside, his work evaluated as a scissors-and-paste job. When interest in narrative did enter the world of Gospels-study, it did so first with reference to the Gospel of Mark, but only in the waning years of the twentieth century.[7]

From early on, Matthew attracted special attention, with the result that the early centuries of the church saw the production of commentaries on this Gospel. However, Luke was regarded less for its narrative presentation of Jesus' ministry, and more as an arsenal of episodes from which favorites might be drawn. Luke's story of the birth of Jesus is a case in point, but one could also point to the Christian use of the parables of the Good Samaritan or the Prodigal Son – all texts typically sundered from their narrative service within the Third Gospel. Removed from their Lukan cotexts, these accounts and parables could be situated in and made to serve other narratives, including those supporting Western individualism (thus deemphasizing community) or evangelism (as a practice segregated from social witness). Indeed,

---

6 Augustine, *De consensu evangelistarum* 1.2.4.
7 On the history of interpretation of the Gospel of Mark, see William R. Telford, "Mark, Gospel of," in *A Dictionary of Biblical Interpretation* (ed. R. J. Coggins and J. L. Houlden; London: SCM; Philadelphia: Trinity, 1990), 424–8.

Robert Wuthnow has documented how recitation of the so-called Parable of the Good Samaritan, displaced from its narrative location in the Gospel of Luke, has generated charitable behavior in American public life,[8] but this "Good Samaritan effect" neither embodies the arresting quality of Jesus' parable (how could it, without the larger Lukan narrative influencing how it is read?) nor grows out of the deeply formed wisdom promoted within the Third Gospel. The Acts of the Apostles provided the chronological mannequin on which to drape the clothing of Pauline biography, but the possibility that Luke might be chronicling the growth of the church and extension of its mission in a way that pressed forward a narrative–theological agenda seems not to have been exploited.[9]

If the church has traditionally expressed little concern for the Gospels as narratives, this may be the consequence of the eclipse of narrative concerns by hermeneutical interests of another kind. That is, interest in the narrative forms of biography or historiography – in which the Gospels and Acts appear – has fallen prey to other interests. For example, take the Gospel harmony, which reduces the multiple, narrative witnesses to the significance of Jesus' life, death, and resurrection to a single voice. A single narrative – rather than the four that comprise our Gospel collection – could be useful against the barbs of those detractors who queried the competing voices of the fourfold Gospel witness. A single Gospel harmony could also prove instrumental in the task of initiating new converts into the church's story, and serve the church's interest in a synthesis of the story of Jesus for its ongoing theological task. In the latter half of the second century, Tatian worked material from the Gospels of Matthew, Mark, Luke, and John, like a mosaic, into a single narrative framework, and the result of his efforts, the *Diatessaron* (i.e., "[one Gospel] from the four") remained influential into the fifth century. Even with the ascendancy of the

[8] Robert Wuthnow, *Acts of Compassion: Caring for Others and Helping Ourselves* (Princeton, N.J.: Princeton University Press, 1991).
[9] As in so many areas of the contemporary study of Luke-Acts, the noteworthy exception was Henry J. Cadbury, *The Making of Luke-Acts* (London: Macmillan, 1927; reprint ed., Peabody, Mass.: Hendrickson, 1999).

fourfold Gospel, however, impulses toward harmonization continued. In the early eighth century, the Venerable Bede produced homilies on Gospel texts, working as though each narrative was cut from the same cloth as the other without attending to the particular perspective of any single evangelist.[10] In the sixteenth century, Calvin wrote a series of commentaries on each of the biblical books, except the Gospels of Matthew, Mark, and Luke. He commented on these last three in a synthetic way, not with regard to the discrete witness each has to the life of Jesus, but with reference to a composite picture of Jesus that Calvin was able to produce from the Synoptic Gospels. Those engaged today in the quest of the historical Jesus similarly bypass the narrative character of the individual Gospels, preferring instead to re-create, from sometimes wildly divergent databases of material, their own accounts of Jesus.

Further illustrations of how study of the Gospels has proceeded without reference to the narrativity that defines their character could be garnered from the commentaries that adorn our shelves. The classic work on the Third Gospel by Joseph Fitzmyer is a good example.[11] Completed in 1985, it marked the pinnacle of redaction–critical study of the Gospels, but in more than 1,600 pages of erudition, Fitzmyer treats pericope after pericope of the Third Gospel, each in relative isolation, with little attention paid to the significance of the narrative location of that pericope, and thus with only the barest of attempts to account for narrative coherence. For Fitzmyer, Luke's Gospel bears witness to a plotline, but one focused on the path of developing tradition – from historical events (Stage One) through tradition history (Stage Two) to final inclusion in Luke's Gospel (Stage Three).

The general lack of critical interest in the narrative character of the Gospels and Acts comes as no surprise when we recall early impulses toward modern, critical scholarship from the eighteenth century.

---

[10] In fact, Bede's homilies followed a "narrative" of another sort – namely, the narrative plot of the church's calendar (Bede the Venerable, *Homilies on the Gospels* [2 vols.; Cistercian Studies Series 110–11; Kalamazoo, Mich.: Cistercian, 1991]).

[11] Joseph A. Fitzmyer, *The Gospel According to Luke* (2 vols.; AB 28–28A; Garden City, N.Y.: Doubleday, 1981/85).

Though he was not alone, Johann Philipp Gabler was instrumental in voicing the governing assumption of critical biblical scholarship in the modern era. I refer to his view that the timeless theological truths of the Bible come to us buried like nuggets of gold in the dross of his- torically contingent writings[12] – or, as that other eighteenth-century critic, Thomas Jefferson, put it in his attempt to identify in the Gospels the life and morals of Jesus, like "diamonds in a dunghill."[13]

rather n low view of scriptures than,

Not surprisingly, the introduction of attention to the Gospels and Acts as narratives was bathed in polemic. This may be illustrated most stunningly by the juxtaposition of two books by Edgar McKnight. First, he contributed a slim volume on form criticism to the series *Guides to Biblical Scholarship.* Here we find the expected emphases on classifying units of the Gospels by literary form, on tracing each through its period of oral transmission, and identifying for each its setting in life. In a jarring about-face, McKnight's next major pub- lication signaled his essential rejection of the longstanding tradition of locating the meaning of biblical texts in their prehistory. Instead, McKnight's subsequent book named the address of meaning in its title: *Meaning in Texts.*[14] Perhaps more widely known, though, is the influential critique of the then-regnant approach to reading the Bible, the historical–critical method, undertaken by Hans Frei in *The Eclipse of Biblical Narrative.*[15] Even if he paid little attention to the individual narratives of the Gospels themselves, Frei was successful in putting on

[12] John Sandys-Wunsch and Laurence Eldredge, "J. P. Gabler and the Distinction between Biblical and Dogmatic Theology: Translation, Commentary, and Discus- sion of His Originality," *SJT* 33 (1980): 133–58 (138).

[13] Cited in Forrest Church, "The Gospel According to Thomas Jefferson," in Thomas Jefferson, *The Jefferson Bible: The Life and Morals of Jesus of Nazareth* (Boston: Beacon, 2001), 1–32 (17).

[14] Edgar V. McKnight, *What Is Form Criticism?* (GBS; Philadelphia: Fortress, 1969); idem, *Meaning in Texts: The Historical Shaping of a Narrative Hermeneutics* (Philadelphia: Fortress, 1978); cf. idem, *The Bible and the Reader: An Introduc- tion to Literary Criticism* (Philadelphia: Fortress, 1985). Eventually, this would lead to McKnight's interest in reader-response criticism – for example, Edgar V. Mc- Knight, *Postmodern Use of the Bible: The Emergence of Reader-Oriented Criticism* (Nashville, Tenn.: Abingdon, 1988).

[15] Hans W. Frei, *The Eclipse of Biblical Narrative: A Study in Eighteenth and Nineteenth Century Hermeneutics* (New Haven, Conn.: Yale University Press, 1974).

display the limitations of historical–critical treatments of the Gospels, which treated these narratives more as aggregates of miscellaneous data concerning Jesus than as stories that invite a reading from beginning to end.

WHERE IS MEANING TO BE FOUND?

With the dethroning of historical criticism, hermeneutical interests and exegetical methods have proliferated. In recent years, many students of the Bible have learned to catalogue old and new interpretive strategies in terms of where each locates meaning in relation to the biblical text. Three (rather obvious) options have emerged: behind-the-text, in-the-text, and in-front-of-the-text approaches.[16] *Behind-the-text* approaches address the text as a window through which to access and examine the deposit of "meaning." These approaches, then, locate meaning in the history assumed by the text, the history that gave rise to the text, and/or the history to which a text gives witness. *In-the-text* methods recalibrate their focus on the qualities of the text itself: its architecture, consistency, and texture. *In-front-of-the-text* approaches orient themselves around the perspectives of various readers of the text, on readerly communities, and/or on the effects that texts (might or do) have on their readers. In this case, readers do not simply perceive but help to produce meaning. Of course, these three are ideal types that rarely, if ever, appear in such pure forms. Nevertheless, this typology continues to have utility, because our methods align themselves more with one category than another. Where do we locate

---

[16] In part, this reflects the recovery of the critical tradition, which has always been more inclusive than the hegemony of historical criticism (which urged that the only style of reading worthy of the designation "critical" was/is historical criticism) might have allowed us to imagine. Some readings are mimetic in theoretical orientation, others pragmatic, others expressive, and still others objective. Each finds the locus of meaning in its own place – say, in "the universe," in "the work," in "the artist," or in "the audience" – and so each in its own way is "critical" insofar as each is concerned both theoretically and performatively with validity in interpretation. See M. H. Abrams, *The Mirror and the Lamp: Romantic Theory and the Critical Tradition* (Oxford: Oxford University Press, 1953); Hazard Adams, ed., *Critical Theory since Plato* (rev. ed.; Fort Worth, Tex.: Harcourt Brace Jovanovich, 1992).

meaning? The history behind the text? The text itself? Those persons
and communities doing the reading?

Given this typology, narrative criticism is self-evidently an in-the-
text approach. However, we would be mistaken to assume that the
practice of narrative criticism of the Gospels and Acts must be defined
in terms of its narrow emphasis on the perspective contained within
and transmitted by the text itself, as if narrative criticism were merely
a matter of apprehending the text as a kind of sealed container of
meaning. This is true for at least four reasons:

(1) The Gospels and Acts are narratives within narratives. Narratives
are constructed through a reversal of cause–effect relations. Knowing
how things turned out, narrators go back in time, in search of causes.[17]
In the case of the Gospels and Acts, the problem of a beginning is the
quest for a starting point capable of supporting, even funding, the
significance allocated to Jesus and the mission of his followers. This
issue is raised immediately by the opening verse of the Gospel of
Mark, ἀρχὴ τοῦ εὐαγγελίου Ἰησοῦ Χριστοῦ υἱοῦ θεοῦ, usually rendered, as in the New Revised Standard Version (NRSV), as a title
or heading: "The beginning of the good news of Jesus Christ, the
Son of God." But this translation is potentially misleading because
it suggests that Mark's own narrative is this "beginning of the good
news" – a reading that violates both the grammar and theology of
the Second Evangelist, as recent commentators have observed. Robert
Guelich helpfully translates, "The beginning of the gospel concerning Jesus Messiah, Son of God, as written by the prophet Isaiah . . . ."
R. T. France adopts a more traditional translation, analogous to the
NRSV, but underscores nonetheless, with Guelich, that the beginning

---

[17] Cf. Edward W. Said, *Beginnings: Intention and Method* (New York: Basic, 1975), 50;
Hayden White, "The Question of Narrative in Contemporary Historical Theory,"
in *The Content of the Form: Narrative Discourse and Historical Representation* (Baltimore, Md.: The Johns Hopkins University Press, 1987), 26–57. This claim regarding
"narratives" is appropriate to the sorts of writings we have with the Gospels and
Acts, concerned as they are with events in the world, but not with all narratives.
In fictional writing, for example, the narrative might "write itself" as it tumbles
toward an unforeseen closure; see the discussion in Gary Saul Morson, *Narrative
and Freedom: The Shadows of Time* (New Haven, Conn.: Yale University Press, 1994).

of the good news does not lie with the advent of Jesus, but with the prophet Isaiah.[18] The ongoing story within which the Gospel of Mark is located – which helps to give the story of Jesus' ministry its significance, and which is itself shaped by Mark's presentation of Jesus – has its roots in the divine promise of liberation of Israel from the bondage of exile as this is anticipated in the prophet Isaiah. That is, locating "the beginning of the gospel" in Isa 40, Mark lays bear his presupposition that the narrative he is about to develop has as its conceptual framework that larger story of Exodus, Exile, and New Exodus.[19]

For the other Gospels, too, the textual point of beginning (i.e., chapter one, verse one) is not really the beginning of the story. Matthew's first two words are βίβλιος γενέσεως, "the book of origins" (NRSV: "the genealogy"), a parallel to Gen 2:4 and 5:1, by which the evangelist points to the consummation in Jesus' advent of the purpose of God in creation. The depths of meaning of the story of Jesus cannot be plumbed without engagement with the very beginning, nor without reference to Abraham and David, Jesus' ancestors (Matt 1:1), and Jesus' ancestral heritage, which Matthew traces back to Abraham (1:1–17). The Acts of the Apostles does not suffer for lack of a "beginning" because it is the second of the two books, Luke-Acts (Acts 1:1). What of the beginning of Luke-Acts? Just as the story of the early church (Acts) is inscribed into the story of Jesus (Luke), so the story of Jesus is written into the story of Israel's Scriptures, particularly the story of Abraham. In Luke's birth narrative (Luke 1:5–2:52), multiple and rotund echoes of the Abraham tradition can be heard. Luke's narrative, then, is a self-conscious continuation of the redemptive story, in which divine promises to Abraham are shown not to have escaped God's memory but indeed to be in the process of actualization in the present.[20] The Fourth Gospel expands the horizons even further.

---

[18] Robert A. Guelich, *Mark 1–8:26* (WBC 34A; Dallas: Word, 1989), 3–14; R. T. France, *The Gospel of Mark* (NIGTC; Grand Rapids, Mich.: Eerdmans, 2002), 49–53. See also Joel Marcus, *Mark 1–8* (AB 27; New York: Doubleday, 2000), 141–9.

[19] See more fully, Rikki E. Watts, *Isaiah's New Exodus and Mark* (WUNT 2:88; Tübingen: Mohr Siebeck, 1997).

[20] Joel B. Green, "The Problem of a Beginning: Israel's Scriptures in Luke 1–2," *BBR* 4 (1994): 61–86.

Here, the story of Jesus cannot be appreciated fully without reference to the beginning of the cosmos, and before: "In the beginning was the Word, and the Word was with God, and the Word was God" (John 1:1).

Each in its own way, the Gospels and Acts self-consciously pick up the story in midstream and write the next chapter of the ongoing work of God. Each in its own way, these NT narratives demonstrate the problem inherent in a methodology focused simply on the qualities of the text itself: its architecture, its consistency, and its texture. These texts invite, even require, critical engagement with what they do not so much narrate as presuppose.

(2) *Both theologically and from the perspective of genre criticism, the Gospels and Acts are narratives with external, historical referents.* "Genre criticism," the discernment of a text's genre and exploration of the implications of genre, is an important first step in the interpretation of any text. As familiar patterns of speech, genres promote certain effects by inviting certain readerly practices. It almost goes without saying that, as first-century documents, the Gospels and Acts will participate in broad literary forms available to first-century writers and audiences. Working with these texts is not always a simple task for later audiences for whom Matthew or Mark may not fit familiar patterns. Nevertheless, even readers arrayed across a spectrum measured in degrees of competence are able to attain a certain amount of satisfaction.[21] This is because, in the most simple sense, we recognize that these texts belong to the larger category of writing we know as narrative. And narratives of all sorts call for a common set of interpretive practices.[22] But this is not enough.

[21] Cf. Glenn W. Most, "Generating Genres: The Idea of the Tragic," in *Matrices of Genre: Authors, Canons, and Society* (ed. Mary Depew and Dirk Obbink.; Cambridge, Mass.: Harvard University Press, 2000), 15–35 (17–18); Joseph W. Day, "Epigram and Reader: Generic Force as (Re-)Activation of Ritual," in *Matrices of Genre*, 37–57 (38–9).

[22] So, for example, when discussing *The Art of Biblical Narrative*, Alter works with authors as chronologically and generically disparate as Homer and Dickens. Despite the obvious differences separating historical from fictional narratives, their narrators face analogous problems and employ similar literary conventions, and, at some level, their readers follow comparable interpretive protocols; cf. esp. Wallace Martin, *Recent Theories of Narrative* (Ithaca, N.Y.: Cornell University Press, 1986), 72–5.

Within their milieu in the first-century Mediterranean world, the Gospels and Acts comprise recognizable transformations of two primary, narrative genres. The Gospels of Matthew, Mark, and John follow patterns familiar from Greco-Roman biography, and the Gospel of Luke and Acts of the Apostles, read as a single, continuous narrative, are calibrated within the broad category of Greco-Roman historiography. This is not to exclude precursors within Israel's own Scriptures, of course. The historical narratives of Genesis or 1 Kings, as well as the more focused, biographical material on Elijah and Elisha or on Joseph, suggest the extent to which the Gospels and Acts participated literarily within the biblical tradition of the Jewish people. Nor is it to draw too strict a line between biography and historiography in the Greco-Roman world, as though, say, Mark and Luke should be read in significantly different ways. Biography has as its primary focus a *bios*, a life, whereas historiography locates events on center stage. But in the Roman world of the first century, biography was still the youthful offspring of the more hoary tradition of writing history.[23] However one parses the intermingling of literary traditions and contamination of generic elements in the production of the Gospels and Acts, the point is clear: It is not enough to attend to matters of literary presentation because these forms of narrative have significance in relation to a series of referents – persons and events – outside the text, taken individually and collectively.[24]

Theologically, the same can be said in terms of the witness of the Gospels and Acts. It is not enough to say that these narratives are history-like, or that they have the character of verisimilitude, because they claim more than this. To illustrate, for Luke it is important that

[23] Cf. John Marincola, *Authority and Tradition in Ancient Historiography* (Cambridge: Cambridge University Press, 1997), 19–33; and, more generally, Charles William Fornara, *The Nature of History in Ancient Greece and Rome* (Eidos: Studies in Classical Kinds; Berkeley: University of California Press, 1983). The other major narrative category would have been the (fictional) novel, which also grew out and in imitation of historiography. For the influence of fictional narrative on, say, the Acts of the Apostles, together with the inappropriateness of locating the Gospels and Acts within this generic category, see for example, Niklas Holzberg, *The Ancient Novel: An Introduction* (London: Routledge, 1995).

[24] So Albert Cook, *History/Writing: The Theory and Practice of History in Antiquity and in Modern Times* (Cambridge: Cambridge University Press, 1988), 55.

"the word of God came to John son of Zechariah in the wilderness" at a particular time: "In the fifteenth year of the reign of Emperor Tiberius, when Pontius Pilate was governor of Judea, and Herod was ruler of Galilee, and his brother Philip ruler of the region of Ituraea and Trachonitis, and Lysanias ruler of Abilene, during the high priesthood of Annas and Caiaphas" (3:1–2). Most explicit in its affirmation that history matters is John 1:14: "And the Word became flesh and lived among us."

Undoubtedly, antipathy regarding their historical veracity contributed to the rise of literary approaches to the Gospels and Acts. A principled agnosticism on issues of historical reference thus led to sometimes splendid insight regarding narrative coherence, with extra-textual reference the sacrificial lamb. Thus, it may not be surprising that, in his massive study of *Jesus Remembered*, James Dunn locates his discussion of narrative criticism in his chapter on "The Flight from History."[25] Is it possible to read the Gospels and Acts as narratives without uncoupling historical interests? In an important sense, the answer to this question depends on how those historical interests are defined and their pursuit practiced. In what follows, let me sketch a way forward.

First, we must accept the reality that "History" with a capital "H" does not exist, as Paul Veyne puts it,[26] because the person (or community) responsible for the telling is forever engaged in the making of choices of what to exclude and include, and how to relate one event to another. Decisions are required – and not only for the obvious reason that if everything "were written down, I suppose that the world itself could not contain the books that would be written" (John 20:25), but also to escape the democratization of events whereby nothing has significance because everything is of equal consequence. And yet, decisions involving valuation are inescapably subjective, oriented as they are around particular interpretive aims and set within particular

---

[25] James D. G. Dunn, *Christianity in the Making*, vol. 1: *Jesus Remembered* (Grand Rapids, Mich.: Eerdmans, 2003), 94.

[26] Paul Veyne, *Writing History* (Middletown, Conn.: Wesleyan University Press, 1984), 26.

chains of cause-and-effect. Historians are concerned with what they and their communities deem to be significant among the many events that might have been recorded, and in the relationships among the events that are recounted. As Veyne explains:

Facts do not exist in isolation, in the sense that the fabric of history is what we shall call a plot, a very human and not very "scientific" mixture of material causes, aims, and chances – a slice of life, in short, that the historian cuts as he [sic] wills and in which facts have their objective connections and their relative importance.... Then what are the facts worthy of rousing the interest of the historian? All depends on the plot chosen.... In history as in the theater, to show everything is impossible – not because it would require too many pages, but because there is no elementary historical fact, no eventworthy atom. If one ceases to see the events in their plots, one is sucked into the abyss of the infinitesimal.[27]

To take a single, crucial example: What of the death of Jesus? Would a Latin historian writing, say, at the end of the reign of Tiberius even have heard of Jesus or his execution? If he had, would he have had reason to mention it? If he had, would it be for any purpose other than to document how Rome dealt with those who threatened *pax romana*? And if the Gospels and Acts relocate Jesus' crucifixion from a footnote in the annals of history to its status as an epoch-making event, is this not because they locate it within different interpretive horizons – that is, within a different plot? The narrative representation of historical events thus locates events in a web of significance. If this significance is analyzed theologically, this does not make the consequent narrative any less historical.[28]

The paradox of history/writing, as Albert Cook labels it, is that verification and narrative come into focus in every single sentence. Historiographical accounts cannot be peeled, layer after layer, as if

---

[27] Veyne, *Writing History*, 32–3.
[28] C. T. McIntire helpfully shows how the segregation of history and theology was and is predicated on a dichotomy alien both to premodern thinking and to virtually all religions, which present "the religious as a way of life, and not as something that can be confined to a special private realm or removed from life altogether" ("Transcending Dichotomies in History and Religion," *History and Theory* 45 [2006]: 80–92 [86]).

the interpretive husk could be separated from the historical kernel, because each sentence (each layer, so to speak) has both an interpretive and a documentary force. For Cook, this means that history/writing must be experienced and judged globally and cannot be disconfirmed event-by-event.[29]

Second, we would invite transformed perspectives on historiography as "mimesis." This is because memory of persons and events is being formed long before the historian appears on the scene to take up the twin tasks of research and narration. Oral history represents and shapes the community of memory. History-telling precedes and constrains history/writing. Moreover, memories are in a perpetual state of flux, being surfaced or suppressed, held or lost, in relation to their perceived importance. Interpretive commitments, rooted in and expressed by communities of memory, are already in play. There is something provocative and suggestive, then, about Wolfgang Iser's observation that, in narrative, the referent of the work of mimesis has shifted from "the world out there" to "perception of the world out there."[30] As a result, the pressing question becomes, on the microlevel: How is this event related causally to that one? And, on the macrolevel: What end is served by narrating the story in this way (rather than some other)? The task of a narrative–critical reading of the Gospels and Acts thus locates itself less in relation to concerns with validation and more in terms of signification.

This means that, at least theoretically, the story of Jesus and the Jesus movement might have been related differently by different writers possessed of different interests, when compared with what we have in the NT. Even if one were to use the same database provided us by Matthew or Luke, an alternative narrative could be spun, with a different order, a different teleology, a different set of cause-and-effect relations. Presuming the availability of communities of memory, the only necessary limitation on the range of potential narratives that might have been

---

[29] Cook, *History/Writing*, 55–72.
[30] Wolfgang Iser, *The Fictive and the Imaginary: Charting Literary Anthropology* (Baltimore, Md.: The Johns Hopkins University Press, 1993), 281–303.

generated is the requirement, placed on all history/writing, of shaping an account that leads to the present. That is, history/writing must demonstrably account for what now is. The possibility of other narratives presses the importance of taking seriously the narratives we do have: Why these (and not some other)?

Third, we would take seriously the status of the Gospels and Acts as cultural products, as narratives that speak both out of and over against the worlds within which they were written. They participate in, legitimize, perpetuate, and criticize the worlds within which they were generated. As Stephen Greenblatt has observed, texts exist in a relationship of constraint and mobility with their cultural contexts, as authors assemble and shape the forces of their worlds in fresh ways that both draw upon and point beyond those cultural elements.[31] These narratives have ongoing significance in part because of their capacity to speak beyond the limitations of their own historical particularity. Yet, as cultural products, the fullness of their voice is determined by that very particularity. Taking seriously this aspect of the historicity of the Gospels and Acts allows us a sharper image of how, say, Mark or John pursued the task of shaping the identity of a people through shaping their writings at the same time that it militates against our impulses toward domesticating these narratives by locating them within our own cultural commitments, as though they embodied and authorized our cherished dispositions.

Fourth, we would attend more pointedly to the persuasive art of these narrators – Matthew, Mark, Luke, and John – and particularly to what each has chosen to include, how each has ordered his material, and into what plotline each has inscribed the whole. Like any historiographer or biographer, Mark's work presumes not only the availability of facts, but a storyline into which Mark's story is inscribed. This storyline includes a beginning and end, expectations and presumptions, which tacitly guide the actual narrativizing process. Accordingly, these

---

[31] See Stephen Greenblatt, "Culture," in *Critical Terms for Literary Study* (ed. Frank Lentricchia and Thomas McLaughlin; Chicago: University of Chicago Press, 1990), 225–32.

narratives would materialize again as subjects in the work of interpretation, as narratives in general are wont to do. That is, the Gospels
and Acts would be heard again to extend their invitation for people
to embrace *this* story as their own, to indwell it, to be transformed in
living it.

(3) *From the moments of their generation and first actualization, the
Gospels and Acts, as with narratives more generally, had intended effects.*
By referring to these narratives as invitations, I have already prepared
the way to counter the relegation of these texts to the category of
information or the idea that our reading of them as narrative must
be dispassionate. Narrative is not just story but also action – as James
Phelan puts it, "the telling of a story by someone to someone on some
occasion for some purpose."[32] Of course in making this claim, we are
departing from perspectives on historical study and history/writing
deeply (if often unconsciously) indebted to the philosophy of history
famously articulated by Leopold von Ranke (1795–1886). Not want-
ing to pass judgment on the past, he wanted simply to report "*wie
es eigentlich gewesen*": "how it actually was." Though dated and end-
lessly critiqued, historical inquiry in this tradition has long outlived
von Ranke, motivated especially by a desire to emulate the investigative
commitments and techniques of the natural sciences. This tradition
stands at odds with early Christian sensibilities regarding the narrative representation of historical events derived from the tradition of
history/writing in the Greco-Roman world and historical narrative in
the Jewish tradition (both Old Testament and Hellenistic Jewish historiography). From their Jewish precursors, Christians drew especially
their interests in the advancement of historical events in the service
of God's purpose, the role of historical narrative in instruction, the
repetition of patterns in characters and events, and the punctuation
of history/writing with the awareness of God's continued presence.
"Histories," pioneered by Herodotus (*ca.* 484–425 BCE) but standard-
ized in the work of Thucydides (*ca.* 460–400 BCE), were concerned not

---

[32] James Phelan, *Narrative as Rhetoric: Technique, Audiences, Ethics, Ideology* (Colum-
bus: Ohio State University Press, 1996), 8. See further, David Lowenthal, *The Past
Is a Foreign Country* (Cambridge: Cambridge University Press), 1985.

merely with reporting events but with describing and explaining their sequential development. Taking the claims of ancient historians at face value, moderns have tended to characterize Greco-Roman historiographers as dispassionate investigators who rejected the place of myth, the supernatural, and the use of rhetorical tools and aims. To the contrary, their practices reveal their concern to persuade their audiences to a particular reading of the past, and their concomitant employment of a variety of means for sanctioning their accounts – including reference to divine intervention and the supernatural, imitation, and patterns of prediction and recurrence.[33] To shape the identity of their audiences, to legitimize a movement, and to demonstrate continuity with the past – such aims as these characterize these texts, whose character then must be understood in rhetorical terms, as acts of persuasion, and not simply with regard to literary artistry.

(4) *The Gospels and Acts are "open texts" – that is, they both invite and require the participation of their audiences.* Umberto Eco theorizes two broad categories of texts, based on the type of cooperation requested of the reader. In the first, a text offers multiple possible occasions for predicting what is happening and why, but at each stage the text asserts its own rights by requiring a certain predetermined view of what is true. This is a "closed text," the parade example of which Eco offers Ian Fleming's James Bond novels. These narratives follow a stereotypical structure that allows for no reading other than that Bond will get the girl and conquer the villain. Other readings are foreclosed by the rules of the game inscribed in this narrative world.[34] The open text, by contrast, encourages – indeed, expects – an interactive dynamic between text and audience, because the author has left the arrangement of some elements of the work to the reader. For Eco, texts like the Gospels and Acts are characterized by the invitation for readers "to make the work" together with the author. They are rendered meaningful in personal

---

[33] See Clare K. Rothschild, *Luke-Acts and the Rhetoric of History: An Investigation of Early Christian Historiography* (WUNT 2:175; Tübingen: Mohr Siebeck, 2004).

[34] See Umberto Eco, *The Role of the Reader: Explorations in the Semiotics of Texts* (Advances in Semiotics; Bloomington: Indiana University Press, 1979), 33–4, 144–72.

and communal performance. These narratives, then, are capable of a range (though not an infinite number) of possible valid meanings, depending on who is doing the reading, from what perspectives they read, and what reading protocols they practice.[35]

In short, on account of the need to reach beyond the Gospels and Acts for a suitable point of beginning, for theological reasons, due to considerations of genre, and because of their character as persuasive texts requiring the participation of their audiences in the process of meaning-making, narrative criticism of the Gospels and Acts cannot be reduced to consideration of literary devices and textual artistry. Historical, readerly, and theological concerns must be integrated with elements typically associated with narratology – theme, plot, characterization, point of view, and so on.

WHAT IS A NARRATIVE?

When it comes to defining "narrative," we may find it easier to admit, "We know it when we see it." This is because the term itself is contested.[36] By attending to this question, we begin to get a better sense of what is involved in the critical study of narrative.

(1) Narrative is a defining feature of the human family by which we make sense of our lives. Scientist-theologian Anne Foeret refers to humans as "*Homo Narrans Narrandus* – the storytelling person whose story has to be told," who tells stories to make sense of the world and to form personal identity and community.[37] Embodied human life performs like a cultural, neuro-hermeneutic system, locating (and thus making sense of) current realities in relation to our grasp of the

---

[35] In addition to Eco's *Role of the Reader*, see his book, *The Open Work* (Cambridge, Mass.: Harvard University Press, 1989), and the more recent *Interpretation and Overinterpretation* (Cambridge: Cambridge University Press, 1992).

[36] See, for example, Prince, *Narratology*, 58–60; and, more fully, Michael J. Toolan, *Narrative: A Critical Linguistic Introduction* (London: Routledge, 1988), 1–11; H. Porter Abbott, *The Cambridge Introduction to Narrative* (Cambridge: Cambridge University Press, 2002), 12–24.

[37] Reported in S. Jennifer Leat, "Artificial Intelligence Researcher Seeks Silicon Soul," *Research News and Opportunities in Science and Theology* 3, no. 4 (2002): 7, 26 (7).

past and expectations of the future. To speak thus of past, present, and future is already to frame meaning in narrative terms. This is not so much a statement about exegetical method, but rather about narrativity as an essential aspect of our grasp of the nature of the world, and of human identity and comportment in it. "To raise the question of narrative," observed Hayden White, "is to invite reflection on the very nature of culture and, possibly, even on the nature of humanity itself."[38] Although our recognition that humans are basically hard-wired to render events meaningful within a narrative frame does not yet provide for us a definition of "narrative," it does point toward important ingredients of such a definition.

(2) *Narrative locates events in a temporal frame characterized by cause-and-effect relations.* In his *Poetics*, Aristotle wrote of a narrative whole as possessing a beginning, middle, and end. At one level, this assumes narrative progress from one point to the next, organizing the progression of events through time. At another, this narrative progression transcends the passing of time in order to claim some sort of meaningful, even necessary, set of relationships among the events that, in narrative, order time. The beginning is not simply the first thing to be narrated, but the thing before which nothing is necessary and after which something naturally follows. The end is not simply the last thing to be recounted, but something that is naturally after something else (generally as its necessary consequence) and that requires nothing after itself (*Poetics*, 1450^b).

(3) *Narrative is a particular performance of a story.* It follows that integral to narrative is the particular ordering of events by which significance accrues to those events. This is the classic distinction made by Seymour Chatman between "story" and "discourse" – that is, between the "what" (events, characters, settings) and the "how" (the organization of those events, characters, and settings in a particular telling).[39]

---

[38] White, *Content of the Form*, 1.
[39] Seymour Chatman, *Story and Discourse: Narrative Structure in Fiction and Film* (Ithaca, N.Y.: Cornell University Press). Mieke Bal distinguishes among three levels: fabula, story, and text (*Introduction to the Theory of Narrative* [Toronto: University of Toronto Press, 1985]). See the discussion in Toolan, *Narrative*.

Put simply, the same event can mean different things, depending on the narrative within which it appears. Luke locates Jesus' preaching in Nazareth at the outset of his public ministry in a way that has attracted from numerous Lukan scholars the label "programmatic." Accordingly, Luke 4:16–30 lays the groundwork for Jesus' preaching and healing throughout the Gospel, and anticipates the words and deeds of Jesus' witnesses in the Acts of the Apostles. Mark, on the other hand, locates Jesus in Nazareth in his sixth chapter, well into the public ministry of Jesus, where it serves above all to document evolving hostility toward Jesus and the marginalization of Jesus within the narrative. Another example: What are we to make of Jesus' work of exorcism? Placed within one narrative, when Jesus casts out demons it proves that he is in league with Beelzebul, Lord of the Flies, the prince of demons (Luke 17:15). Placed within another, when Jesus casts out demons it proves that he operates within the sphere of God's own Spirit and puts into play the dominion of God against evil (Luke 17:20).

(4) Narrative progression serves a (single) narrative aim. Finally, it follows that a narrative *telos* or "aim" guides the selection and organization of the elements of story. The identification of a beginning, middle, and end and the structuring of settings, actors, and events in a web of causal relations are teologically determined. They serve an overall purpose that presses the narrative forward toward resolution (or denouement). We may discern within a narrative various currents and countercurrents – and these bear witness to the elasticity of narrative, the hospitality of narrative to multiple agenda – but, in narrative study, these are tamed in relation to the overall purpose of the narrative. For example, we might recognize within the Gospel of Mark heightened concern with the character of discipleship or a concern with the basis of the Gentile mission, but neither of these interests explains the whole of the Markan narrative. What is it that drives the narrative forward from its prologue – which maps the ministries of John and Jesus in relation to Isaianic good news – to its denouement in Jesus' cross and empty tomb? Thinking in these terms urges narrative critics to account for (A) the overarching divine purpose at work in

and through the Gospel of Mark, (B) the division within the text of those characters who embrace (or help) this purpose versus those hostile to (or who oppose) that purpose, and (C) how the Gospel of Mark functions for its readers and hearers to invite and form from among them "helpers" of this divine agenda.

ELEMENTS OF NARRATIVE

Narrative study insists on attention to a range of elements by which a typical narrative text accentuates or deemphasizes. One kind of reader experiences the text under the tutelage of the narrator generally without realizing what is in the foreground, midground, or background. Another kind of reader, the narrative critic, is interested not only in the mere "that" of the text's emphases but also in "how" the text serves to generate particular readerly experiences. Thus, narrative criticism includes a complex process of attending to the dynamics or artistry of the Gospels and Acts. In what follows, I will sketch a short list of some prominent elements.

(1) *Sequence:* In the day-to-day world as we experience it, events occur without any necessary relationship from one to the next. Retrospectively, we sometimes venture to say that event X led to event Y, or event Z was the probable outcome of event A. The narrative portrayal of historical events is not so subtle. In narratives, the organization or structure of events puts on display the ordering of time and documents a particular understanding of how one event not only leads to, but is causally related to, the next. Audiences, then, experience narratives less as a chronological sequence of events (because there is often no necessary *temporal* relationship of one event with the next, and at times events are manifestly told out of chronological order [e.g., flashbacks or flashforwards]) and more as a progression of events with the next understood in light of the preceding. What comes first is at least implicitly understood to provide the grounds for the second, and so on. Read thus in sequence, narrative order is a form of persuasion. For example, we know that at Jesus' baptism "the Holy Spirit descended upon him" (Luke 3:22) and that, in his inaugural address

Jesus interpreted his baptism as a vocation and empowerment for mission with the words of Isa 61:1–2; 58:6: "The Spirit of the Lord is upon me . . . " (Luke 4:18–19). From this narrative point forward, we understand that Jesus operates in the sphere of the Spirit even though his experience of the Spirit is almost never again mentioned (Luke 10:21; cf. 5:17; Acts 10:38).

(2) Staging: Where is the scene located? What is the significance of this geography or architecture within the word of the narrative? Is the scene delineated in terms of an important time – perhaps in relation to other scenes or in terms of an important day, like Passover or Sabbath? For example: "Now he was teaching in one of the synagogues on the sabbath" (Luke 13:10). (What is the significance of synagogues? Sabbath? In Luke, what happens when Jesus is in the synagogue on a Sabbath? See Luke 4:16–30.) Where are the characters located in relation to other characters? If we imagine ourselves as recording this scene with a camera, who or what is in the center of the picture? In relation to whom or what does the action develop? Who or what is in focus? Out of focus? For example: "And just then there appeared a woman. . . . When Jesus saw her, he called her over and said . . . " (Luke 13:11–12). (Here Jesus is the center of attention, and at his invitation the woman shares this center.)

(3) Time: We measure time in the world in seconds and minutes or decades and centuries, with each day or month the same length as the next. In narratives, though, the flow of time is manipulated for the sake of emphasis. Time can be rushed, so that days or weeks or even months can be captured in a single verse, as in this summary statement: "So he continued proclaiming the message in the synagogues of Judea" (Luke 4:44). Conversely, time can be elongated, as in the account of Jesus' suffering and death, so that the goings-on of only a few hours take up two entire chapters (Luke 22–23). Compare this with the opening two chapters of Luke's Gospel, which cover some thirty years of real time.

(4) Characterization: Narrators sometimes *tell* us about a character, as with the character reference by which we learn that Zechariah and Elizabeth are blameless yet childless in Luke 1:5–7. Narrators sometimes give us insight into a character by *showing* us their actions, words, and responses, as with Mary's response to Gabriel in Luke 1:38.

Narrators sometimes guide our understanding of characters through the reports of others (especially if we have learned from the narrative to trust the reports of those others). If Jesus, a reliable character in the Gospel of Luke, reports on the problematic behavior of the scribes (e.g., Luke 20:46–47), we are inclined to think less of scribes. If unnamed spectators refer to Zacchaeus as a "sinner" (Luke 19:7), we can be sure that these onlookers have evaluated Zacchaeus in these terms, but we might wonder if we should trust their evaluation. (Alternatively, we can take at face value that Zacchaeus is wealthy and a ruler among toll collectors and that he is a "son of Abraham" – evaluations provided by the narrator [Luke 19:2] and by Jesus [Luke 19:9], respectively.)

(5) *Perspective:* As this last illustration already hints, narratives typically present diverse, sometimes competing perspectives on what is unfolding. Jesus, according to the divine voice that speaks at his baptism and transfiguration, is God's son – and this divine perspective is shared by Jesus himself (e.g., Luke 2:49; 3:21–22; 9:35; 10:21–22). To others though, Jesus is "a great prophet" (Luke 7:16); John the Baptist or Elijah or even God's Messiah (Luke 9:19–20); or a false prophet and pretender to the throne (Luke 23:1–5). In the Gospels and Acts, we find that the perspectives of God (and divine beings as well as the Scriptures, when interpreted rightly), Jesus, and the narrator are – generally speaking – a single reliable perspective and that they provide the perspective by which other points of view are judged.

(6) *Insider Information:* In the case of the Gospels and Acts, the narrator is typically heard but not seen. Only rarely does the narrator slip out from behind the curtain to address the audience directly. When they do, however, it is to assist their audience's understanding while at the same time bringing the audience more fully into the confidence of the narrator. Luke, of course, begins his Gospel by addressing his audience directly (1:1–4) before merging into the background. He reemerges from time to time – for example, to give his audience background concerning the requirements of Torah or to explain why Jesus' disciples were unable to make sense of his passion predictions (cf. Luke 2:22–23; 9:45; 18:34).

(7) Intertextuality. Though of a different sort, another kind of insider information is provided in the Gospels and Acts through the pervasive presence of quotations, allusions, and echoes of Israel's Scriptures. Readers of Luke's account of Jesus' raising of a dead son and returning him to his mother (7:11–17), for example, will recall that Jesus had already interpreted his mission with reference to Elijah's having been sent to "a widow at Zarephath in Sidon" (Luke 4:25–26), itself a reference to the account in 1 Kgs 17:8–24 in which Elijah revived the only son of a widow and returned him to his mother. Intertextuality implicitly adds layers of theological significance not only to the scenes where they can be discerned but also, in terms of the unfolding story of God, to the narrative as a whole.

In practice, the list of literary devices to which narrative critics might attend is practically endless,[40] with the result that the most important task of the narrative critic is not so much to learn a kind of literary technology but to develop literary sensibilities. "A close reading of the text" refers especially to the exercise of just these sorts of sensibilities: slowing down in order to hear the text (rather than force it into the role of the puppet through which the interpreter-as-ventriloquist is able to speak in terms sometimes quite foreign to the text), to savor its dynamics, and to be surprised by its artistry.

READING A NARRATIVE ACCOUNT: LUKE 16:19–31[41]

The Lukan Cotext

For the narrative critic, this parable presents two immediate challenges, both of which have to do with narrative cotext – that is, with

---

[40] See, for example, Bernard Dupriez, *A Dictionary of Literary Devices* (Toronto: University of Toronto Press, 1991) (500+ pages of entries). Although more circumspect, Resseguie follows his discussion of narrative elements with a convenient list of question for guiding a narrative–critical reading (*Narrative Criticism*, 341–44).

[41] In what follows, I draw on Joel B. Green, *The Gospel of Luke* (NICNT; Grand Rapids, Mich.: Eerdmans, 1997), esp. 598–610; for narrative readings, see also James A. Metzger, *Consumption and Wealth in Luke's Travel Narrative* (BIS 88; Leiden: Brill, 2007), 132–57; Outi Lehtipou, "Characterization and Persuasion: The Rich Man and the Poor Man in Luke 16.19–31," in *Characterization in the Gospels*, 73–105.

the location of this parable within the larger Lukan narrative. The first issue has to do with whether v. 19 is an appropriate point to begin our analysis. Although it is self-evident that v. 19 ("There was a rich man . . . ") is the beginning of the parable, narrative criticism is not particularly enamored with considerations of literary form (or form criticism) in determining narrative organization. In fact, one of the distinctive characteristics of narrative as a mode of discourse is its hospitality to all sorts of literary forms, the ingredients by which it shapes a beginning, middle, and end. Rather than literary form, we are on the lookout for textual signals indicative of narrative arrangement, such as topographical or temporal markers, the introduction of new characters, or changes in speaker or audience.

In this case, Jesus' parable, which opens in v. 19, does not begin a fresh section within the narrative, but is actually a continuation of a narrative section that began in v. 14. According to 16:1, Jesus addresses his disciples with a parable, "There was a rich man. . . . " In spite of Luke's clear identification of Jesus' audience as his disciples, in v. 14 Luke unveils the previously hidden presence of a secondary audience, the Pharisees – who, having heard "all this" (vv. 1–13, at least), "ridiculed him."[42] With v. 15, Jesus initiates a response to the Pharisees, a response that continues through 16:31, after which Jesus addresses his disciples again (17:1). This means that the parable in 16:19–31, from a narrative–critical perspective, does not stand on its own but must be interpreted as part of Jesus' response to the Pharisees (i.e., 16:14–31).

---

[42] This sort of indeterminancy around audience is characteristic of Luke's narration in the Travel Narrative (9:51–19:48) – contra Luke Timothy Johnson, *The Gospel of Luke* (SP 3; Collegeville, Minn.: Liturgical, 1991), 164–65; Jack Dean Kingsbury, *Conflict in Luke: Jesus, Authorities, Disciples* (Minneapolis, Minn.: Fortress, 1991), 56, 124; David B. Gowler, "'At His Gate Lay a Poor Man': A Dialogic Reading of Luke 16:19–31," *PRSt* 32 (2005): 249–65 (252). Even when Luke identifies audiences with some specificity, others are often present, however implicitly, as in this case. The parade example of this sort of ambiguity is Peter's own inability earlier to identify to whom Jesus is directing his speech: "Lord, are you telling this parable for us or for everyone?" (12:41). This is actually a clever narrative device, because it allows Jesus to instruct his followers regarding discipleship, for example, while leaving open the possibility that his instructions will be heard and embraced by would-be followers as well. Similarly, in the present text, we might say that Jesus addresses his words to Pharisees *and to others for whom it is true that they are "lovers of money"* (16:14).

The second issue is closely related to the first because, in effect, with
vv. 19–31 we have two narrators speaking at once. At one level, of course,
Jesus narrates what is traditionally called the parable of the Rich Man
and Lazarus. This provides the basis for most traditional approaches
to the interpretation of this parable, because it allows students of Jesus
and the Gospels to sunder the parable from its narrative setting in Luke
and to treat it in relation to other settings – typically, within someone's
(but not Luke's) understanding of Jesus of Nazareth and often in
relation to parallel accounts in Greco-Roman and/or Second Temple
Jewish writings.[43] For the narrative critic, however, irrespective of its
origins or background, the parable now comes to us embedded within
the Lukan narrative, with the result that we now hear the evangelist's
voice in the voice of Jesus. Jesus' narration serves Luke's narrative
aims. Hence, although issues of background are not unimportant, the
most significant context for reading the parable is the one provided by
Luke himself – namely, the Lukan narrative and how it understands
and portrays the world.

Luke then presents the Pharisees as eavesdroppers on Jesus' instruction to his disciples in 16:1–13. The presence of the Pharisees is actually
no surprise because, together with experts on the law ("scribes"),
the Pharisees were already present as Jesus' audience in Luke 15 – a
chapter comprised primarily of Jesus' defense of his ministry against
their grumbling and indictment (15:1–3). Moreover, most of Luke 14 is
set within the home of a leader of the Pharisees (14:1–24). Generally,
Luke's portrayal of the Pharisees has marked them as unrelentingly
hostile toward Jesus. They monitor and question his behavior (5:17, 21,
30; 6:2, 7; 11:53) and accuse him of blasphemy (5:31). Yet Luke portrays
some Pharisees as hospitable toward Jesus, even though the manner
of their hospitality betrays their failure genuinely to welcome him
and his message (7:36; 11:37; 14:1). Moreover, some Pharisees side with

---

[43] Important studies include Ronald F. Hock, "Lazarus and Micyllus: Greco-Roman
      Backgrounds to Luke 16:19–31," *JBL* 106 (1987): 447–63; Richard Bauckham, "The
      Rich Man and Lazarus: The Parable and the Parallels," *NTS* 37 (1991): 225–46;
      William R. Herzog II, *Parables as Subversive Speech: Jesus as Pedagogue of the
      Oppressed* (Louisville, Ky.: Westminster John Knox, 1994), 114–30.

Jesus against Herod (13:31).[44] At the same time, Luke provides us with a few generalizations about the Pharisees, all of which are inescapably negative: together with the legal experts, they reject God's purpose for themselves (7:30); they are overwhelmed with greed and status seeking, and their concerns with ritual purity are a sham (11:39–44); and they are like "yeast" in their lack of insight into God's character and purpose (i.e., in their "hypocrisy," 12:1).[45] Luke's characterization of the Pharisees in 16:14 is similarly unfavorable. They sneer at Jesus (ἐκμυκτηρίζω, *ekmyktērizō*, referring to something like "turning their noses up at him"). This response is grounded, first, in what they had heard and, second, what kind of people they are. What had they heard? Clearly, Luke's "all this" includes Jesus' message to his disciples in vv. 1–13, but could also include 15:1–32 and even 14:1–24 – that is, the antecedent teaching of Jesus directed at the Pharisees to which the Pharisees have not yet been given opportunity to respond. Indeed, all of this material is similar thematically in its concern with Jesus' emphasis on hospitality toward and almsgiving on behalf of the poor versus the Pharisees' emphasis on status seeking and purity. Their grumbling (15:2) has thus given way to derision (16:14). What kind of people are they? Luke characterizes them as "lovers of money." Note, this does not mean that first-century Pharisees were wealthy; we have no historical evidence to support such a claim. Nor in most

---

[44] For Luke's characterization of the Pharisees, see for example, David B. Gowler, *Host, Guest, Enemy and Friend: Portraits of the Pharisees in Luke and Acts* (Eugene, Ore.: Wipf & Stock, 1991); idem, "Luke 16:19–31," 252–5; John A. Darr, *On Character Building: The Reader and the Rhetoric of Characterization in Luke-Acts* (LCBI; Louisville, Ky.: Westminster John Knox, 1992), 85–126; idem, "Irenic or Ironic? Another Look at Gamaliel before the Sanhedrin (Acts 5:33–42)," in *Literary Studies in Luke-Acts: Essays in Honor of Joseph B. Tyson* (ed. Richard P. Thompson and Thomas E. Phillips; Macon, Ga.: Mercer University Press, 1998), 121–39. My representation of the evidence resists an overly static approach to Luke's characterization of the Pharisees, allowing for the possibility of a positive response from a (or some) Pharisee(s); see further, Joel B. Green, *The Theology of the Gospel of Luke* (NTT; Cambridge: Cambridge University Press, 1995), 70–5.

[45] In Luke's Gospel, ὑποκριτής (*hypokritēs*, "hypocrite") and ὑπόκρισις (*hypokrisis*, "hypocrisy") do not refer so much to "play-acting" or "insincerity" as to "lacking insight into God's character and purpose." More generally, see Job 34:30; 36:13; 2 Macc 6:21–25; 4 Macc 6:15–23; Gal 2:11–14; Heinz Giesen, "ὑπόκρισις, ὑποκρίνομαι," *EDNT* 2:431–2; *TLNT* 3:406–13.

instances does Luke's narrative present them as wealthy. In fact, "lovers of money" says nothing about the Pharisees' annual income or net worth, either historically or within the Lukan narrative itself. "Lovers of money," rather, is a slur used to label others as concerned with self-aggrandizement and, thus, as false teachers or false prophets. Indeed, note how, later in the narrative of Luke-Acts, Paul presents himself to the Ephesian elders in garb other than that of a money-lover: "I coveted no one's silver or gold or clothing" (Acts 20:33). Elsewhere in the NT we read that "the love of money is a root of all kinds of evil" (1 Tim 6:10), and we find in the ancient Mediterranean world other witnesses to this sentiment.[46] Luke has repeatedly *shown* the Pharisees to be so consumed with the maintenance and advancement of their social standing that any lingering concern for the plight of the poor would be negated (e.g., 11:39–43; 15:1–2). Luke now *tells* his readers the same thing, summarizing in a single expression – "lovers of money" – the rapacity of the Pharisees, their lack of care for the marginal, and their hyperconcern with status seeking.

Historical–critical analysis has little to say about the significance of vv. 15–18 in this setting. Howard Marshall's comments (from a redaction–critical perspective) are representative: "The connection of thought at this point in the section is far from obvious. . . . It may be best to assume that Luke was governed by the order of the material in his sources, and that he has put it together as best he could, but not with complete success."[47] Working under the assumption of literary congruousness, the narrative–critical approach pushes harder in its attempt to find cohesion in this larger unit, 16:14–31. Marshall's perspective is guided by his decision that vv. 14–15, 19–31 are concerned

---

[46] For example, 1 Thess 2:5–6; 1 Tim 6:5–10; 2 Tim 3:2; Tit 1:11; Philo *Praem.* 127; Dio *Discourses* 32:9–11; 35:1; 54:1–3; Epictetus *Discourses* 1, 9, 19–20; Lucian *Timon* 56. See Halvor Moxnes, *The Economy of the Kingdom: Social Conflict and Economic Relations in Luke's Gospel* (OBT; Philadelphia: Fortress, 1988), 6–9; Johnson, *Gospel of Luke*, 249–50.

[47] I. Howard Marshall, *The Gospel of Luke: A Commentary on the Greek Text* (NIGTC; Grand Rapids, Mich.: Eerdmans, 1978), 624; cf. Fitzmyer, *The Gospel According to Luke*, 2:1111–21.

with the theme of "wealth," whereas the theme of vv. 16–18 is "the law." From a narrative perspective, however, fundamental to this interchange between Jesus and the Pharisees is the parable's climax, when Abraham asserts, "They have Moses and the prophets; they should listen to them" (v. 29). However emphatic Jesus' message regarding wealth and poverty might be in vv. 14–15, 19–31, the overarching theme of this passage is heeding Moses and the prophets – or, to paraphrase: Who interprets dependably and embodies faithfully Israel's Scriptures? Understood in this way, vv. 15–18 make a great deal of sense in this cotext, for they demonstrate that the Pharisees have distanced themselves from the very law they thought to uphold. Jesus is not the one who transgresses the law; they are. This is not because they set out deliberately to live outside the law, but because, failing to grasp God's aims, in their very advocacy of the law's significance they misconstrue its meaning. If only they grasped the nature of the good news of the kingdom Jesus proclaims, they would see that his mission upheld (and not abrogated) the law (vv. 16–17). Of course, from Jesus' programmatic address in 4:16–30 we know that this mission, itself grounded in Scripture, moves onto center stage "the poor" as recipients of the good news.

How do vv. 15–18 make clear the Pharisees' ironic distance from the purpose of God revealed in Israel's Scriptures? In the Scriptures, the sense of "abomination" (16:15) extends to immoral financial dealings and the act of remarrying a divorced woman (Deut 24:4; 25:16) as well as to idolatry more generally (e.g., Isa 1:13; 66:3). Similarly, an Essene text, the Damascus Rule, names "three nets" by which Israel is snared (CD 4:14–16:1): fornication (and particularly a lax rendering of the Mosaic legislation concerning divorce), wealth, and profaning the temple (explicated in terms of false prophecy and failure to understand and keep covenant with God). Not coincidentally, these are the very issues at stake in Jesus' response to the Pharisees in vv. 15–31. Ironically, these categories reappear later in the narrative, when Jesus portrays a Pharisee praying in the temple, thanking God he is not like those who swindle others, who are unjust, or who commit adultery

(18:9–14). There, Luke observed that Jesus' parable was told "to some who trusted in themselves that they were righteous and regarded others with contempt" (18:9); similarly, here, Jesus asserts of the Pharisees, "You are those who justify yourselves in the sight of others" (16:15).[48]

Of course, more is at stake with regard to the Lukan cotext of 16:19–31 than Luke's portrayal of the Pharisees. More will become clear momentarily, when we delve into the parable itself, but a wide-angle lens encourages contemplation of some of Luke's larger interests. Thus, for example, Luke 16:19–31 appears in an extended segment of the Gospel that begins in 13:10, a lengthy section of the Gospel occupied with boundary-drawing typified by a question like, "Lord, will only a few be saved?" (13:23), or an exclamation like, "Blessed is anyone who will eat bread in the kingdom of God!" (14:15). This sets up well the emphasis on judgment and afterlife in 16:19–31.

In Luke 13:23–30, presence at the end-time meal spells participation in the kingdom of God. In Luke 14:1–24, meals establish "in-group" boundaries and embody values pertaining to status and purity. In these texts, the table is an expression of kinship, and dining manifests concerns for honor and acceptance. Jesus, of course, has a habit of flaunting these social and religious protocols, repeatedly eating with the "wrong" people – wrong, that is, as defined by the usual standards – and encouraging others to do the same (e.g., 5:20–32; 7:34, 36–50; 14:1–6, 13, 21, 23; 19:1–10). Meals foster existing bonds of community, but in Luke's portrayal, Jesus teaches in word and deed that table fellowship ought to establish new and unexpected relations. Who will sit at the table of the kingdom banquet? Not those who assumed that the end-time banquet was included among their just desserts; not the "first," but the "last" (13:23–30). Whom should one invite to one's luncheons (14:12–14)? Not those whose very presence at the table would bolster the host's status in the community, not those capable of reciprocating with invitations of their own, but the poor, the crippled, the blind, the lame. Use what you have to include the peripheral people among your closest friends, Jesus advises, so that you may be welcomed into

---

[48] Cf. Moxnes, *Economy of the Kingdom*, 148–50.

eternal homes (16:1–13). This sets up well the twinned emphases on wealth/poverty and eating in 16:19–31, as well as the prominent motif of eschatological reversal.[49]

Characterization in Luke 16:19–31

The most transparent literary device of this parable is the extraordinary parallelism by which its two main characters are portrayed. Both are males and, eventually, both end up in Hades, but here the list of their similarities comes to an abrupt end. We can follow our comparison of the two by moving through the three temporal stages of the parable.

- Life in This Age, Separated by a Gate (vv. 19–21)
  - The one man is rich, the other poor. On the one hand, these terms are a barometer of the separation between these two figures, with the poor man portrayed as one of society's "expendables" (downwardly mobile, on the verge of death),[50] the other as a wealthy landowner with an estate and the power and prestige accompanying landed wealth. On the other, already within the Third Gospel, Luke has filled in his own lexicon for terms like "poor" and "rich," with "poor" understood in terms of the marginal to whom the grace of God is directed (e.g., 4:16–30; 6:20–26; 7:18–23) and the "rich" portrayed as those with significant resources at their disposal who nonetheless fail to consider the plight of others, whose relationships are defined in terms of equality and mutuality, and who have received in this life whatever comfort they are to receive because over them is pronounced divine judgment (e.g., 1:51–53; 6:20–26; 12:16–21).[51]

---

[49] See further the reflections of John Paul Heil in his analysis of the relation of 16:19–31 to the meal scenes prior to this account (*The Meal Scenes in Luke-Acts: An Audience-Oriented Approach* [SBLMS 52; Atlanta: Society of Biblical Literature, 1999], 142–5).

[50] See Gerhard E. Lenski, *Power and Privilege: A Theory of Social Stratification* (2nd ed.; Chapel Hill: University of North Carolina Press, 1984), 281–4.

[51] See Joel B. Green, "Good News to Whom? Jesus and the 'Poor' in the Gospel of Luke," in *Jesus of Nazareth: Lord and Christ: Essays on the Historical Jesus and New*

- The one man is a wealthy landowner, dwelling in a gated compound; the other has no home but has been tossed (βάλλω, *ballō*) at the wealthy man's gate. (His apparent lack of mobility suggests that the poor man is crippled.)
- The one man is dressed in purple and fine linen; the other is covered with sores. This emphasis on external appearance is a reminder that, in the ancient world, clothing expressed not only status and wealth but *who one was*. Clothing put on display who one was in relation to others, so that the wealthy man's portrait is one of royal status and opulence in the extreme.[52] Conversely, the lack of any mention of clothing on the part of the poor man contributes to his inhumanity, and the detail about his sores underscores not only his miserable health but also his persistent state of uncleanness.
- The one man feasts sumptuously everyday; the other "longed to satisfy his hunger with what fell from the rich man's table." In an economy where the wealthy might afford to kill a calf only occasionally, here is a man whose resources are beyond imagination. Compare this with the other, whose only desire in this parable is to have his share of the scraps, otherwise scavenged by dogs, that fell from the table (cf. 15:16).
- The wealthy, well-clothed, well-fed man has no name, but the other is called "Lazarus."[53] The importance of this marker of status is highlighted, first, by the observation that, in the NT Gospels, he alone has a name. He is no longer a poor man, but a man with a name – personalized, as one with whom we might empathize. The importance of the name is found, second, in the

---

Testament Christology (ed. Joel B. Green and Max Turner; Grand Rapids, Mich.: Eerdmans, 1994), 59–74.

[52] See Klaus Berger, *Identity and Experience in the New Testament* (Minneapolis, Minn.: Fortress, 2003), 40–3; and, especially on related concerns of wealth and status, Gildas Hamel, *Poverty and Charity in Roman Palestine, First Three Centuries* C.E. (Berkeley: University of California Press, 1990), 57–93.

[53] The importance of his being called by his name stands irrespective of whether we can assume on the part of Luke's audience an awareness of the meaning of the name "Lazarus" in Hebrew: "God helps."

history of interpretation, which apparently could not allow the marginal person Lazarus to have a name while the person of privilege lacked one. Thus, some interpreters have named him "Dives" (from the Latin *dives*, for "rich [man]," v. 19). But for Luke he is nameless. He is "no one," true, but he is also "anyone" – anyone, that is, whose love of money allows a gate to remain shut to the plight of the needy. The unfolding calamity of the wealthy man with no name is marked by his knowledge of the name of this poor man at his gate, "Lazarus," to whom he never extended hospitality (v. 24).

- Death (v. 22)
  - The one man died and was buried; the other died (and apparently was not buried). Proper burial was critical among Romans and Jews.[54] The story's description of the pitiful, disgraceful state of Lazarus reaches its zenith in the implication that his body was left shamefully exposed, available for scavengers (like dogs, v. 21).
  - The reversal of fortune for the poor man, portended already in his being called by name in v. 20, is also and decisively signaled in v. 22: "he was carried by the angels to the bosom of Abraham."[55] In their former lives, Lazarus lay at the gate of the wealthy estate owner; in the afterlife, the wealthy man must "look up" (v. 23) to see Lazarus in his exalted position.
- The Afterlife, Separated by a Nontraversable Great Chasm (vv. 23–31)
  - The one man is tormented in Hades; the other is in Abraham's bosom. How could both be in Hades? This is because Second Temple Judaism supported no single view of Hades. Evidence from the wider world of Luke would allow for readings of Hades as the general abode of the dead; the abode for all of the dead prior to the Final Judgment; the abode of the wicked and the righteous prior to the Final Judgment, during which time punishments and rewards are already being assessed; and exclusively the place

---

[54] For the curse associated with a lack of burial, see Deut 28:25–26; Jer 16:1–4.
[55] My translation; the NRSV leaves κόλπος (*kolpos*, "bosom") untranslated in v. 22.

of punishment for the wicked.[56] A similar perspective is found in the *Testament of Abraham*, usually dated to the first century CE. In ch. 11 of the *Testament* we read of two gates, one for the righteous who enter Paradise (or heaven, 20:12), the other for sinners destined for destruction and eternal punishment, with judgment occurring (as in Luke's parable) at the moment of death and not at the end.

- Already present in Abraham's bosom, where "... there is no toil, no grief, no mourning, but peace, exultation and endless life" (*T. Ab.* 20:14),[57] Lazarus shares in Abraham's celebrated hospitality and participates in the heavenly banquet (see Luke 11:22–30). The rich man begs for a drop of water (16:24).
- The one man claims to be a child of Abraham; the other is a child of Abraham. The rich man refers to Abraham as his "father" (vv. 24, 27, 30), a relationship Abraham apparently affirms in v. 25 ("child"). However, the Lukan narrative has already taught us that a genuine filial relationship with Abraham is not a matter of ancestry: "Bear fruits worthy of repentance. Do not begin to say to yourselves, 'We have Abraham as our ancestor'; for I tell you, God is able from these stones to raise up children to Abraham. Even now the ax is lying at the root of the trees; every tree therefore that does not bear good fruit is cut down and thrown into the fire" (3:8–9). That is, Abraham's children are known for embodying

---

[56] Cf. the helpful summary in Richard Bauckham, "Hades, Hell," *ABD* 3:14–15; and especially, idem, "Descents to the Underworld," in *The Fate of the Dead: Studies on the Jewish and Christian Apocalypses* (NovTSup 93; Leiden: Brill, 1998), 9–48; idem, "Early Jewish Visions of Hell," in *The Fate of the Dead*, 49–80; and idem, "Visiting Places of the Dead in the Extra-Canonical Apocalypses," in *The Fate of the Dead*, 81–96, Bauckham notes that Hades and paradise are within sight of each other in such texts as 4 Ezra 7:85, 93, just as Gehenna and paradise appear within sight of each other (4 Ezra 7:36–38; 1 En. 108:14–15). See also Outi Lehtipun, *The Afterlife Imagery in Luke's Story of the Rich Man and Lazarus* (NovTSup 123; Leiden: Brill, 2007).

[57] ET in E.P. Sanders, "Testament of Abraham: A New Translation and Introduction," in *Old Testament Pseudepigrapha* (2 vols.; ed. James H. Charlesworth; Garden City, N.Y.: Doubleday, 1983/85), 1:871–902 (895).

in their lives the faithfulness of Abraham and for putting into practice his legendary hospitality to strangers (see 19:9). But this rich man has not shared what he had with the one present at his gate who had nothing (see 3:10–11!), so he finds himself "cut down and thrown into the fire." For his part, Lazarus typifies what it means to be a child of Abraham in Luke's narrative – those defined by others as outside the boundaries of God's chosen and thus in need of God's mercy, yet the very ones for whom God's fidelity is manifest.[58]

- Abraham himself best summarizes the eschatological reversal recounted in the parable: "Child, remember that during your lifetime you received your good things, and Lazarus in like manner evil things; but now he is comforted here, and you are in agony" (v. 25). Previously, the rich man could have traversed the gate separating him and Lazarus; having failed to do so, he now finds himself separated by a gulf that cannot be crossed. Hear the programmatic words of Mary's Song: "He has brought down the powerful from their thrones, and lifted up the lowly; he has filled the hungry with good things, and sent the rich away empty" (1:52–53; cf. 6:20–21, 24–25).

We might wonder about the basis of the eschatological judgment that leaves the rich man in a state of torment and the poor man in a state of bliss. After all, we find in Israel's Scriptures the common view that wealth is a sign of God's blessing for the faithful, with poverty an expression of God's judgment on the disobedient (e.g., Gen 24:35; Deut 28; Job). Taken on its own terms, though, the parable provides no moral evaluation of either character. The one is wealthy, the other impoverished, but neither is depicted in the parable itself as either wicked or pious. Locating the parable within its Lukan cotext, however, we see immediately that wealth and poverty attract not only

---

[58] See 1:54–55; 3:7–9; 13:10–17; Joel B. Green, "Jesus and a Daughter of Abraham (Luke 13:10–17): Test Case for a Lucan Perspective on Jesus' Miracles," *CBQ* 51 (1989): 643–54 (651).

economic (or status-oriented) but also moral assessments. As we have seen, Luke has already developed canons by which to evaluate persons described in these terms:

Blessed are you who are poor, for yours is the kingdom of God. Blessed are you who are hungry now, for you will be filled. . . . But woe to you who are rich, for you have received your consolation. Woe to you who are full now, for you will be hungry. (6:20–25)

The tragedy of the rich man achieves a new level of irony in the closing verses of the parable, when he asks of Abraham that he send Lazarus back as a witness to his brothers. The rich man is not without compassion after all, but his compassion is tightly boundaried. We hear in the background Jesus' instruction in 14:12–14:

He said also to the one who had invited him, "When you give a luncheon or a dinner, do not invite your friends or your brothers or your relatives or rich neighbors, in case they may invite you in return, and you would be repaid. But when you give a banquet, invite the poor, the crippled, the lame, and the blind. And you will be blessed, because they cannot repay you, for you will be repaid at the resurrection of the righteous.

Here is a man who has been banqueting on a daily basis, but his circle of table companions does not extend to someone like Lazarus – poor, perhaps crippled. His concern extends only as far as his brothers, but this is not nearly far enough. After all, according to the canons of interpretation provided in 14:12–14, their relationship with one another is characterized by mutuality of concern and reciprocity of economic exchange, a mutuality and reciprocity that lie beyond the realm of possibility for the rich man and Lazarus. Having failed to invite to his table the pitiful man at his gate, the one who could never repay him, the rich man now receives no reward at the resurrection of the righteous.

If we remember that, in 14:12, "the one who had invited him" was a leading Pharisee, we will also be reminded that Jesus' parable in 16:19–31 is similarly addressed to Pharisees, "lovers of money." In this cotext, then, the rich man has as brothers these Pharisees who had grumbled against Jesus on account of his hospitality to the socially marginal (15:1–2) and who had ridiculed his teaching about the faithful use of the wealth of this world in caring for the poor (16:14). This is Jesus' indictment against them: In neglecting the poor, they have snubbed the will of God so plainly expressed in the Scriptures.

Hearing the Scriptures

Let me make two final observations. First, in his final words, Abraham remarks that those who do not listen to Moses and the prophets will not be convinced if someone were to rise from the dead (16:31). Of course, from the standpoint of the Lukan narrative, someone, Jesus, has risen from the dead. What might seem a rather pessimistic closing statement for the parable, then, is transformed into new possibilities. This is because, for Luke, the resurrection of Jesus becomes the hermeneutical lens for understanding Israel's Scriptures. Indeed, in Luke 24 the mantle Jesus takes up is that of biblical interpreter. "Then beginning with Moses and all the prophets, he interpreted to them the things about himself in all the scriptures" (24:27; cf. 24:44–49).[59] The resurrection itself introduces no new vision of God's will, but clarifies the nature of God's design and so provides the needed perspective from which to read the Scriptures.[60]

Second, we should note that the interchange between Jesus and the Pharisees does not reach a satisfying closure. Their exchange is cut short as Jesus turns in 17:1 to address his disciples. Is their conflict resolved? Heightened? Within the narrative, we do not know how they heard Jesus, nor how they might have responded to his words of challenge and warning. It is easy enough to think the worst of the Pharisees, and to imagine the worst, of course, but these are the same Pharisees about whom Jesus warns his disciples in 12:1: "Beware!"

---

[59] See further, Richard B. Hays, "Reading Scripture in Light of the Resurrection," in *The Art of Reading Scripture* (ed. Ellen F. Davis and Richard B. Hays; Grand Rapids, Mich.: Eerdmans, 2003), 216–38 (229–31).

[60] Significantly, then, later in the Lukan narrative, "testimony to the resurrection of the Lord Jesus" is correlated with care of the needy (Acts 4:32–34).

Why would he thus warn his followers unless he knew of their own inclinations toward attitudes and behaviors that for Luke deserve the label "Pharisaic"? That is, the line between disciples and Pharisees is permeable. The message in 16:14–31 is open-ended, then, so that it might serve as a challenge and warning to would-be followers both in and outside of the narrative – that is, to Luke's own audience, too. How is our hearing of Moses and the prophets?

5

↓

A Latino Perspective

Justo L. González

REFLECTIONS ON THE PRIORITY OF METHOD

As I reflect on the task assigned to me, and how I would organize the present chapter, I am immediately struck by the contrast between how the chapter is to be organized, and the manner in which I actually do biblical interpretation. According to the instructions received – and which I shall follow – each chapter is to begin with a general discussion on a particular method and how it might be applied to the Gospel of Luke, and then use a text either from Luke 16 or Luke 20–21 as an illustrative example of how the method works. This seems quite logical, straightforward, ideologically neutral, and universally acceptable. To our modern mind, it makes more sense to move from the general to the particular, from theory to practice, and from method to application.

However, one of the basic things we have discovered as Latinas and Latinos[1] doing theology and biblical interpretation is that such

---

[1] When speaking or writing on this subject, I am repeatedly asked what is the correct term, whether "Latino" or "Hispanic." As is so often the case with such terms, both have been imposed from outside – the first by the French, seeking hegemony over the newly independent Iberian colonies, and the latter by the U.S. Bureau of the Census. Furthermore, both have been used by some Hispanic/Latinos to exclude others. Therefore, both are inadequate – just as to call all English-speaking white people in the United States "Anglos" is quite inadequate. One further factor to be taken into account is that "Latino" and "Latina" are gender-specific terms, whereas "Hispanic" is not. Thus, to speak of "Latinos" may tend to exclude women in a way in which the term "Hispanic" does not. And the phrase "Latina theology" is most

seemingly neutral and universally acceptable procedures often imply values and approaches that are not as neutral as they seem. In this particular case, the suggested structure itself implies that method precedes practice; that first one studies and decides what procedures to employ in reading Scripture, and then one applies those procedures to specific texts. It is an approach that favors the general over the particular, and the theoretical over the practical. First one determines the theory, and then one puts it into practice.

This approach has dominated several disciplines throughout most of modernity – and this is particularly true of theological studies. Most of us who are engaged in the various fields of theological studies – theologians, biblical scholars, historians, homileticians – or in the enterprise as a whole, take for granted that this approach is normative: candidates for ordained ministry should first receive their theological education, and then put it into practice. Within the curricula of theological education, this is reflected in the predominance of theoretical courses in the first years of seminary, and the move toward the more practical in the latter years. During the first year in seminary, one studies theology, Bible, history, and the like. Courses on preaching, counseling, church administration, and such are usually postponed until at least the middle of the course of studies, and particularly the senior year. This is also reflected in the polity of most major denominations in the United States, for which the normal route to ordained ministry, once one has ecclesiastical endorsement, is to go to seminary, and then be ordained. Because this general approach does not always work within our church and society, several denominations have developed routes into ordained ministry that allow people to practice at least some aspects of that ministry while proceeding with their studies. It is significant, however, that these approaches are often called "alternate routes," thus implying that the normal and normative

commonly understood as theology done by Latinas – that is, by Hispanic women – whereas "Hispanic theology" does not have such connotation. In any case, rather than focusing on names, I prefer to focus on the issues behind such names, and therefore I use them as synonyms, often alternating between them.

way of doing things is to move from theory into practice, and from studies into ministry.

Although all of this makes sense from a particular point of view, as Hispanics engaged in ministry or seeking to enter the ranks of ordained clergy, it is clear to us that it tends to marginalize Latino and Latina leadership, which generally follows such supposedly "alternate" routes. In the Latino church, only a very small percentage of pastors attend seminary at all, and only a fraction of these follow the supposedly normative route of studying before practicing ministry.

Although this is not the place to continue discussing how all this affects or should affect our understanding of ministry and training for it, or our theological curricula, I find it necessary for readers of this essay to understand why I find it difficult to begin with questions of method or of approach and then move to a specific passage. It is not just a question of hermeneutical theory, but also of the actual practice of ministry and of biblical interpretation.

BIOGRAPHICAL REFLECTIONS

Furthermore, an approach in which methodological questions precede the actual practice of biblical interpretation does not adequately reflect the way I have come to my present position, nor the experience of most Latinos and Latinas. I was reading and interpreting Scripture long before I even heard such a word as "hermeneutics" or had any thought about methods of biblical interpretation. At this point, I must claim my own biography and make it clear to the reader that my approach to Scripture reflects that biography. Therefore, although it may resonate with other Latino and Latina approaches, I cannot claim that it is typical of all Latinos.

There are at least three points at which my biography is parallel to other Latinos but differs substantially from many others: generation, denomination, and gender.

Regarding generation, I came to the United States as an immigrant who was already a Protestant. This means that my previous experience in my country of origin (Cuba) has profoundly affected the way I read Scripture. I grew up before the Second Vatican Council, at a time when the Roman Catholic Church seemed to take for granted that Latin Americans were by nature and by right Roman Catholics, and that Protestantism was an anomaly. (This is a notion to which many Roman Catholic leaders in Latin America still cling, even after Vatican II and after statistics show that in their own countries Protestantism is growing at an explosive rate.) In that setting, the Bible had a twofold function: It was employed within the life of my church as a guide to worship, belief, and practice; and it was also employed beyond the church itself as a tool for doctrinal debate. When someone criticized me for being a Protestant – which happened almost daily – I would respond by confronting them with the Bible. I was taught to use the Bible among my peers at school as a tool for evangelization – which at that point meant turning nominal or actual Roman Catholics into Protestants. I still remember – with a mixture of both shame and pride – how as a teenager I would seek out priests and nuns to argue with them. The more open the debate was, the better! And the basis for that debate was always the Bible, whose authority my opponents also acknowledged, but which from my perspective they ignored. Now, half a century later and in a completely different setting, I look back at those debates and often bemoan my bellicose attitude, my rigid dogmatic stance, and my lack of charity. But I do not bemoan the sense of the authority of Scripture that those formative years left in me. Even as I learned new methods of interpretation, and as I came to different views as to what various texts actually meant, the sense has always remained – that I am dealing with authoritative texts and not simply with another piece of interesting literature. And the sense has always remained that the reading and interpretations of these texts are a crucially serious matter and not just an academic or hermeneutical exercise.

Coming then to live in the United States, the Bible came to play a different role. Now I was no longer in the minority theologically, but I was now an ethnic and cultural minority. Within my own denomination and its institutions, as well as in society at large, I found that I had to prove myself in ways in that were not required of those of the dominant culture and race. I soon learned that when I went to preach at an English-speaking service, people expected me to speak about Cuba and the church there or to inspire them with my life story, but not to preach the gospel, with its promise and demands. Therefore I soon transferred my earlier convictions on the authority of Scripture to my new setting. I had to make it clear that I was preaching not on my own authority but on the authority of the Bible. And something similar was true in my struggles, jointly with other Latino and Latina colleagues, to make my denomination and the church at large take the Latino reality seriously. It was not enough to quote census figures. It was not enough to show that our population was underrepresented in church and academia. It was necessary to show that this was contrary to the word of God.

In all of this, my approach to Scripture tends to differ from that of some of my friends and colleagues who grew up in this country, and against whom Scripture has been quoted repeatedly. In general, we agree on the need to reinterpret Scripture. But they often feel freer than I do to confess that a particular passage is against them, and to seek other sources of authority to support their claims.

On the matter of denominational affiliation, it is obvious that Latinos and Latinas who grew up as Roman Catholics, and still are, do not share my early experiences of using the Bible to argue against a prevailing denomination. Thus, they are more comfortable than I am with theological stances in which Scripture is one of several sources of theology, and in which those other sources help them correct or qualify those passages that may be used against them. Significantly, most Latino commentaries on Scripture in the United States have been written by Protestants, whereas several of the most influential books in other fields have been written by Roman Catholics. Similarly, among Protestant Latinos and Latinas pursuing advanced degrees in the various fields of theology, the greatest number center their attention on the Bible, particularly on the New Testament, whereas this is not true of Roman Catholics.

Finally, I must add a word regarding gender. I have never had the Bible quoted against me as a male in order to keep me down or to limit my possibilities. I have had it quoted against some of my advocacy stands in favor of women, but I am sure that is not nearly as painful as is the experience of women against whom the Bible has been quoted. Latinas often have the experience of having the Bible quoted against them at a variety of levels: their gender, their ethnicity, their culture, and in the case of Afro-Latinas, their race. Thus, in spite of all that I have said previously, I tend to sympathize with claims that the biblical text is biased when it comes to gender – to use the coined words, that it is "patriarchal" or "androcentric." I struggle with those passages that my Latina sisters find most offensive, sometimes finding it difficult to cling to my views on the authority of Scripture, and rejoicing when I find in Scripture texts that affirm women, or texts that can be reinterpreted in ways that are not gender-exclusive. (This may be one of the reasons why I particularly like Luke-Acts, but that is a matter to be discussed later in this essay.)

THE CIRCULARITY OF INTERPRETATION

What I have said previously regarding the inadequacy of an approach that privileges the general over the specific, and the discussion on method over the actual interpretation of concrete texts, does not mean that there is no place for methodological reflection. Method is crucial. It simply is not the only or the best starting point. One does not begin by discussing how to interpret Scripture and then moving on to the actual interpretation. Most of us have begun by reading Scripture with little sense of the role interpretation plays in our reading. In our devotional reading, few of us stop to consider various possible interpretations according to different methods. We read. We interpret. And then we begin reflecting on our interpretation.

Although this is true of most people who grew up within the context of a church, it is particularly true in the Latino church and merits a brief digression to help the reader understand what is in fact the most common Latino approach to Scripture. It is often said that most Latinos are fundamentalists. This is not true. Fundamentalism is a movement born as a reaction to liberalism, and bears all the marks of that origin – particularly in its combativeness. What typically takes place in a Latino context is not so much a fundamentalist as a naive reading of Scripture. Whereas a typical fundamentalist would say, "This has to be so, because the Bible says it, and those who think otherwise are wrong," most Latinos simply say, "This is what the Bible says." Thus, although the content of their reading may be the same – for instance, God created the world in six days – the thrust of that reading is often different. It is true that in recent decades, partly in connection with the Christian right and other such political movements, true fundamentalism has made inroads into the Latino church. But this is for the most part an imported attitude, and not one born within that church itself. Sadly, those who disagree with fundamentalism often fail to see the difference, and thus force Latino and Latina believers into the fundamentalist camp.

Because we begin by the actual reading of Scripture without much consideration of the fact that every reading is an interpretation, and much less of various possible hermeneutical methods, an approach that privileges general method over concrete reading both falsifies our experience and disempowers some of our best, most creative, and most radical readings.

Our own experience – or at least my own – implies a different approach. We begin by reading Scripture. This is the first stage – one that in many cases begins before we are actually able to read Scripture when we have it read to us. At this point, when we read or listen to Scripture, we normally see in it what we have been told it says. Those who have told us that Scripture is authoritative have also explained its meaning to us, and at first we see no difference between the text itself and the interpretation we have received. As a personal illustration, one of my first memories of listening to a sermon had to do with Peter's denial of Jesus. The preacher asked himself how it was that people knew that Peter was one of the disciples. His answer was that knowing Jesus brings such peace and joy that it shows on one's face. I remember leaving church at the end of the service, sitting on the curb across the street, looking at people as they came out, and deciding that not one of them knew Jesus!

Then comes the second step. At some point we begin to suspect that there are other possible interpretations. There may be many reasons for this. We encounter different interpretations. We find that what we have been told is at odds with the rest of Scripture. We have difficulty relating the text to our own life and situation. We discover that the interpreter has left out part of the text. In my own case, with regard to Peter's denial, it did not take long before I decided that what the preacher said made no sense. I knew many truly sincere and faithful Christians – my own parents among them – whose face did not shine. So almost immediately after sitting on the curb across the street, I came to the conclusion that the preacher had made it all up. What he said was not true, and the story must have some other explanation. Because it was not such a crucial matter, I thought little about it for a while. But it did undercut my trust in what the preacher said from that time on!

The next step – and in some ways the crucial one – comes when we actually discover a different meaning in the text, and realize that such a discovery has to do with who we are and where we stand. In my dealing with Peter's denial, this came many years later. I had almost forgotten about the rather silly sermon I had heard long ago. By now I had finished my Ph.D. and was teaching in Puerto Rico. I had been invited to preach a Holy Week series of sermons at a large English-speaking Methodist Church in the United States. I had preached in English frequently, but this was usually to small congregations and in special mission study occasions. Now I was to preach in this large church, and I was afraid that I would not be clearly understood because of my accent. To make matters worse, one of my former professors, a native English-speaker, had just heard me deliver a lecture in English. He had told me that he wished I would work on my accent, because the lecture was very good, but he had to make an effort to understand all that I said. With much trepidation, I began preparing my series of sermons, which were to be based on the events surrounding the passion according to the Gospel of Matthew. I was carefully working on the exact wording of what I was to say, making sure that there were no words that people might have difficulty understanding. When I

came to Peter's denial, I remembered that sermon I had heard long
before and smiled. I certainly would not say that people knew that
Peter was a disciple of Jesus because his face shone! Then suddenly,
the actual text hit me: "the bystanders came up and said to Peter,
'Certainly, you are also one of them, for your accent betrays you.'"
They knew Peter was one of "them" because he had an accent! At that
point I did not know what else to do with the text, but at least it was
clear to me that this was actually in the text itself, and that the reason
why, after having read the text so many times, I now saw it, was my
particular situation, leading me to be concerned with my own accent.
Thus, in this stage of the process one discovers that one's experience
and location – as well as those of one's community – may well open a
text to new meanings and interpretations.

All along these various stages, there is no thought of a method –
or at least no thought of a method other than what we were taught
at school. But soon the insight regarding the importance of the interpreter's location leads one to consider the possibility that there may
be similar hidden meanings in well-known texts. In my own case,
because I had to prepare that series of sermons, I simply continued
working on the story of the passion and soon discovered that the prejudices of Judeans against Galileans play an important role in the texts
about which I had to preach. Later I continued thinking about this
as a crucial hermeneutical tool or perspective. This was particularly
helpful to me as I had returned to the United States, and now found
myself a member of a minority suffering similar prejudices. Significantly, I later discovered that at roughly the same time Fr. Virgilio
Elizondo, a Roman Catholic priest in Texas, and Dr. Orlando Costas,
a Baptist pastor in Connecticut, were working on the same subject of
the marginality of Galilee and Galileans *vis-à-vis* Judea and Judeans.[2]

---

[2] Virgil P. Elizondo, *Galilean Journey: The Mexican-American Promise* (Maryknoll,
   N.Y.: Orbis, 1983). This is a popularized version of Elizondo's more detailed study
   on the subject, which was his doctoral dissertation at the Institute Catholique de
   Paris. Orlando E. Costas, "Evangelism from the Periphery: A Galilean Model," and
   "Evangelism from the Periphery: The Universality of Galilee," *Apuntes: Reflexiones
   teológicas desde el margen hispano* 2, no. 3 (1982): 51–9, and no. 4, 75–84.

It is experiences such as this that lead to the conscious quest for a new method. In my case, the question was: Could it be that the theme of prejudice and marginality could provide valuable insights into the biblical text? What would the Gospels look like if we read them from the perspective of marginality? But even then, one begins developing and applying the method before one is much aware of what one is doing. It is only later, and mostly when one is asked about one's principles of biblical interpretation, that the process leads to reflection on the method itself.

But even then the process has not ended. As one applies the method – consciously or not – to various texts, one begins to discover new dimensions of which one was not aware. Progressively, one becomes aware of dozens of texts that one is still reading with something very similar to the original naiveté of a first reading. As the method is applied to such texts, new dimensions emerge that eventually lead to amplifications and corrections of the method. Thus, the circular process continues. But it is not so much a circle as it is a spiral, for each new turn amplifies the scope of what is being done. In my own case, reading the Gospel of Matthew from a perspective of marginality led to similar readings of other parts of the canon, then to taking into consideration economic marginalization, then to an awareness of similar marginalization on the basis of gender, and so on.

This cycle of interpretation is not exclusive to Latinos and Latinas in the United States. It is the common experience of those against whom the Bible was continually used and who have discovered that Scripture can – and should – be interpreted in a different way, in a way that is empowering and liberating to them. In the case of Hispanics in the United States, we have been very much helped by similar discussions in Latin America, where the priority of praxis over interpretation has been discussed and proposed for more than forty years. When this subject arises, people commonly understand praxis as "practice" but the two are quite different. In common English usage, "practice" has two main connotations: One practices in order to improve what one does – as an athlete or a musician practices, or one practices what one has already learned in theory – as when a physician opens a practice.

Of these two, the first comes closer to what we mean by praxis, for the latter reinforces the common notion that theory precedes practice. Like the practice of the athlete and the musician, praxis is the actual doing and the process of learning and being shaped. Also, as in the case of the athlete or the musician, practice has the result of improving performance, and the same is true of praxis. But praxis is grounded, not on the desire to improve itself, but rather on a commitment to love and justice, and leads to reflection that in turn improves praxis. Thus, praxis is prior to reflection only in the sense that it is not the mere application of theory, but because there is a circular process, praxis leads to reflection, and reflection leads to new praxis.

Juan Luis Segundo has outlined this process in what he calls the "hermeneutical circle," which he summarizes as follows:

> *Firstly*, there is our way of experiencing reality, which leads us to ideologi-cal suspicion. *Secondly* there is the application of our theological suspicion to the whole theological superstructure in general and to theology in particular. *Thirdly* there comes a new way of experiencing theological reality that leads us to exegetical suspicion, that is, to the suspicion that the prevailing interpretation of the Bible has not taken important pieces of data into account. *Fourthly* we have our new hermeneutic, that is, our new way of interpreting the fountainhead of our faith (i.e., Scripture) with the new elements at our disposal.[3]

Although this is too schematic and seems to divide the cycle into two steps, dealing first with theology and then with Scripture, it does help to understand the significance of suspicion in the process. What happened to me in the case discussed previously, of Peter's denial, is parallel to the experience of other Latinos and Latinas who in many ways, as Segundo would say, have had a way of experiencing reality that has led them to suspicion. In the case of scriptural interpretation, such suspicion lies at the heart of the hermeneutical circle and forces us to look closely at the text, always with the suspicion that what we have been told it says is not what it actually says – a suspicion that increases as it is confirmed by our study of one text after another.

---

[3] Juan Luis Segundo, *The Liberation of Theology* (Maryknoll, N.Y.: Orbis, 1976), 9.

Again, in the case of Peter's denial, my initial suspicion did not mean
much beyond a general feeling that the preacher was making things
up. Then, when I returned to the text many years later, my discovery
of the significance of Peter's accent both increased my suspicion and
led me into new inquiries. As those inquiries led me deeper into the
importance of Galilee as a margin that the center sought to ignore,
I found that this model fit more closely with my own experience.
Later, as I read Acts through a similar lens, I began to discover that
the Galilean Twelve had now become a new center, and that Acts was
about new margins. And thus the cycle continues, in part because the
margin tends to become a new center and in part because I find my
own life reflected in that process.

Another way in which Latin American theology has expressed this
circularity is through the triad of "*ver, juzgar y actuar*" — "seeing, judging, and acting." This has been applied by many in Latin America, has
become a typical structure of most programs within the Secretariat for
Hispanic Affairs in the National Conference of Catholic Bishops in the
United States, and is currently used by many Latina and Latino church
leaders of various denominations in the United States. According to
this triad, one *looks* at circumstances and situations with a realistic
eye — one sees, for instance, that police service in a particular neighborhood is deficient. Then one *judges* why this is so — one decides,
for instance, that police service is deficient because City Hall believes
that the residents do not carry much political weight. As a result, one
acts — for instance, one organizes the neighborhood for political action.
But then, precisely because one is acting in a new way, one *sees* new
realities — it is difficult to organize the neighborhood. And so the circle
continues.

In the case of biblical interpretation, this method has been applied
in two different fashions. One uses the Bible as part of the *judging*. After
seeing the existing situation, one looks in Scripture for passages that
help one understand it. The other — which does not exclude the former,
but is a part of it — applies the entire method to Bible study itself. In
this case, *seeing* is simply looking at the text as it is, within its historical,
political, and literary context; *judging* is looking at the text from the

perspective of the present community's context; and the third step is *acting* on that basis. Such acting then leads to a new reading and application – *seeing* and *acting*.[4]

It is precisely this circularity (or perhaps one should say "spirality") of the method itself that is often ignored in more traditional academic circles, and that has led me to open this essay by questioning the notion that it is best to begin with a discussion of methodology and then move to concrete examples.

INTERPRETACIÓN EN CONJUNTO

Although the main example I have given previously is mostly autobiographical, and repeatedly speaks of my experiences and views, one of the main characteristics of Latino biblical interpretation is that it is community-centered. Years ago, when Hispanic theology was barely beginning to develop, Cecilio Arrastía, probably the foremost Latino preacher of the late twentieth century, wrote an article on "*La iglesia como comunidad hermenéutica*" (the church as a hermeneutical community).[5] In that article, he spoke of his own practice as a preacher-pastor. But he was also expressing what is the common experience of many Latinos and Latinas: The Bible is not the possession of an individual interpreter, but rather of a community, and the best biblical interpretation takes place in a community. After all, almost the totality of Scripture was written to be read out loud, before the assembly of the people of God. Biblical interpretation in the privacy of one's study, consulting half a dozen commentaries, is not the first step. The first step is the gathering of the community that hears and interprets the text from its own perspective and out of its own experiences and struggles, and *then* some of its members have the task

---

[4] This is a method I have followed in *Three Months with Matthew* (Nashville, Tenn.: Abingdon, 2002); *Three Months with the Spirit* (Nashville, Tenn.: Abingdon, 2003), dealing with Acts; *Three Months with Revelation* (Nashville, Tenn.: Abingdon, 2004); *Three Months with John* (Nashville, Tenn.: Abingdon, 2005); and *Three Months with Paul* (Nashville, Tenn.: Abingdon, 2006), on Paul's epistles from prison.

[5] Cecilio Arrastía, "La iglesia como comunidad hermenéutica," *Apuntes: Reflexiones teológicas desde el margen hispano* 1, no. 1 (1981): 7–13.

of bringing the wider community into the task of interpretation, by means of commentaries, historical studies, etc. These members of the local community then bring their findings back to it, and thus the dialogue – the interpretation *"en conjunto"* – goes on.

LOOKING AT LUKE FROM "OUT HERE"

All the foregoing is necessary to understand the general characteristics of the Latino approach to the Gospel of Luke, and why the Latino church community finds Luke-Acts so attractive. Naturally, this has much to do with the actual conditions in which Hispanics live, and how they experience both church and society. This is not the place to go into details that can easily be found in any review of the census data. Let it suffice to say that for several decades, negative economic and educational data have consistently been approximately 50 percent higher for Hispanics than for the population at large. Thus, when general unemployment is at 8 percent, Latino unemployment is at 12 percent; and when poverty rates stand at 20 percent the corresponding Latino figure is 30 percent. Although in recent years there has been a slight improvement in official figures, this is more than canceled by the omission of increasing numbers of Hispanics whom the census cannot find or count – mostly because they do not wish to be found or counted – and whose economic and living conditions are often deplorable. As for the church, in every major denomination – Catholic as well as Protestant – there is a significant underrepresentation of Latinos and Latinas in positions of leadership as compared to the percentage of Hispanics in the total populations – and in several denominations, also as compared with the percentage of Hispanics in the denomination itself. Such marginalization has several sources that coalesce in various ways. Obviously, one is economic. Poverty is always marginalizing, and the figures just quoted suffice to show that in this sense Hispanics remain largely marginal to the fiber of both church and society in the United States. Another factor is culture. Latin American culture tends to be undervalued in the United States. Traditionally, Spanish was the language to take if a student wished to have it easy; and this was not because Spanish is easy – it is not – but because standards were lower. A bilingual person who speaks English and German is considered well educated, but a Latino who speaks English and Spanish is doing no more than what is expected. Until recently, most doctoral programs in religion insisted that, in order to meet the requirement of knowing two modern languages besides English, these should normally be German and French. Thus, most Latino doctoral candidates were expected to know at least four modern languages. (No wonder, then, that Hispanics are so underrepresented in the theological academy!) To all of this is added the factor of race. Race is not an objective reality, but a social construct often employed by some to claim superiority over others. In other words, it is not race that results in racism, but rather racism that results in the construction of race. In the United States, race has been constructed in such a way that anyone whose ancestry is not entirely European is classified as nonwhite, and thereby marginalized. In the case of Latinos, all three of these – economics, culture, and race – are seen as sources both of marginalization and of a sense of identity. When all of this is brought to bear on the matter of biblical interpretation, it means that Hispanic readers of Scripture are prompt to see economic, social, and racial–ethnic issues – often all mixed into one.

From such a Latino perspective, the salient characteristic of Luke-Acts is its subversiveness, questioning the existing order and announcing a better one. Or, because the term "subversive" sounds secretive or conspiratorial, perhaps it would be better to speak of the great reversals, or the "upsidedownness" that Luke-Acts announces and exemplifies. This is such a salient characteristic of this literature that once one sees it, it is difficult to understand how it has so often been ignored. This upsidedownness runs through the entire corpus of Lukan literature, so that it would be possible to write an entire commentary pointing out its presence in dozens of passages. Furthermore, it would also be possible to show that this subversive reversal is not Luke's creation, for it shows also in Mark and Matthew. But it is clear that Luke has made it a central theme both in his Gospel and in Acts.

This subversiveness has to do not only with the economic order – rich and poor – but also with cultural distinctions, legal status, gender, culture, and all the usual means and excuses by which people justify the oppression of others.

Because it is impossible to review here all the Lukan material, a few examples should suffice. Probably the one quoted most often is the *Magnificat*, where supposedly meek and mild Mary praises the God who "has scattered the proud in the thoughts of their hearts. He has brought down the powerful from their thrones, and lifted up the lowly; he has filled the hungry with good things, and sent the rich away empty" (Luke 1:51–53). But the theme of reversal, and contrast between the powerful who cannot hear the message and the powerless who do, runs throughout the Gospel. In the story of the nativity in Luke 2, interpreters have often pointed out that Luke places his narrative within its historical setting by mentioning both Augustus and Quirinius. What they often miss, however, is that this reference to the emperor and the governor stands in sharp contrast both to the manger and to the shepherds guarding their flocks at night. The beginning of ch. 2, with its reference to the ruling powers, would lead readers to expect that they will play a crucial role in the narrative, as they do in the existing order. But no, the message comes to some shepherds out "in the fields" – not in Rome, nor even in a city. Reading this story within the Latino community, one cannot avoid relating it both to the settings from which many Hispanics have come, and to their present circumstances. As a group of Salvadoreans said in a Bible study, if a group of poor peasants were sitting around at night in a field in El Salvador, and suddenly a great light shined on them, they would fear that the authorities had been listening to their conversation and their griping about the existing order, and they would certainly need the words of the angel, "Do not fear!" In the present situation of the Latino community in the United States, a census is no more welcome than it was in the ancient Roman Empire. Being counted is not a privilege but a threat. A sudden light shining on one of our gatherings would be an indication that *la migra* – the immigration authorities – had arrived. The good news that the angel proclaims is not only that the way to heaven and life eternal is open, but also that God is intervening, that God has chosen to come to the shepherds rather than to the emperor or the governor.

The passage that is often seen as the beginning of Jesus' public ministry, and setting the tone for his ministry and his message, Luke 4:16–30, is equally subversive. Significantly, most readers in the majority culture fail to see this. If one asks the average Sunday school adult class why Jesus was rejected in Nazareth, the answer will probably be that he was rejected because he claimed to be the fulfillment of the prophecy he had read. But that is not what the text says. In that text, the audience is quite happy, and even thrilled, to learn that the fulfillment of the prophecy is right there before them, that it is one of them. It is when Jesus tells them not to expect any special privileges, and gives the example of God preferring the Syrian Naaman and the Sidonian widow over the people of Israel, that they become enraged and decide to kill him. In other words, he has told them that they are not insiders, as they thought they ought to be. When Latinas and Latinos read this passage, what they find here is not, as is commonly the case within the dominant community, that Jesus is rejected for what he claims to be, but rather that he is rejected by those who had every reason to think that they were at an advantage. This strikes home. Quite often, even in the most open and inviting congregations and denominations, the effort to bring in Hispanics is regarded with a measure of condescension: "We have all the advantages. We grew up in the church. We have an active youth program, a nice fellowship hall, and even a basketball court. Let's be good and offer these facilities to these poor Latinos." But the Gospel of Luke goes far beyond that. The Gospel of Luke – not only in this passage, but throughout – says that those who think they have an advantage must think again, for perhaps the message of joy is coming most clearly to those who, from a worldly standpoint, would seem to have little reason to rejoice.

A similar example has to do with the "sign of Jonah." When asked about this sign, people in most of our "mainline" churches and denominations will say that this has something to do with Jesus being in the tomb for about the same length of time that Jonah was in the belly of the beast. That is certainly part of what Luke says – as well as Matthew. But there is another element in the "sign of Jonah" that often receives much less attention. The sign of Jonah is that the people of Nineveh – outsiders to Israel in the highest degree – will rise up in judgment against those from among the people of Israel who should have known better, and seen what God was doing among them (Luke 11:32). (Significantly, as throughout his Gospel and in the reference to the widow of Zarephath and Naaman the Syrian, Luke [and Matthew] includes a woman, pointing out that "the queen of the South," like the Ninevites, will rise up and judge the people of God.)

Luke's version of the Beatitudes (6:21–26), which seem so nice and mild in Matthew, has a cutting edge of reversal: "Blessed are you who are poor, for yours is the kingdom of God. . . . But woe to you who are rich, for you have received your consolation." "Blessed are you who are hungry now, for you shall be filled. . . . Woe to you who are full now, for you will be hungry." "Blessed are you who weep now, for you will laugh. . . . Woe to you who are laughing now, for you will mourn and weep." "Blessed are you when people hate you, and when they exclude you, revile you, and defame you of account of the Son of Man. . . . Woe to you when all speak well of you, for that is what their ancestors did to the false prophets."

The great reversal is also quite apparent in the parables. The parables of Jesus in Luke – and quite often in the other Gospels – are literally preposterous. Etymologically, preposterous means putting first what should come after: pre-posterous. It is putting the cart before the horse. It is turning the world upside down – the great reversal or "upsidedownness" to which I have already referred. Many of them present clear but shocking words of Jesus: "Some are last who will be first, and some are first who will be last" (Luke 13:30). The lost sheep and the lost coin are more important than the sheep and the coins that were never lost. The prodigal who returns enters the father's feast, and the faithful son who claims he has always done his father's will remains outside. When a man is left for dead by the roadside, it is not the priest or the Levite, but the outcast and unexpected Samaritan, who understands and applies the law of God. When a verdant fig tree

in the middle of a vineyard receives extra care and fertilizer, this is not
a sign that it has been particularly fruitful, but the exact opposite. And
the extra fertilizer, rather than a simple blessing, is also a warning that
the time is short in which to bear fruit. Jesus even goes as far as taking
an employee who cheats on his master as an example for the behavior
of his disciples!

We try to turn the parables into nice and easy and good stories about
common morality, decency, and hard work. And those that we cannot
twist in that direction, we simply ignore. It is not mere coincidence
that all of us have seen numerous stained-glass windows showing a
sower scattering the seed, or a father welcoming the prodigal, or a
shepherd carrying a lost sheep. But we have never seen a window in
which a man with shifty eyes says to another, "Take your bill, sit down
quickly, and make it fifty" (Luke 16:6). Such behavior goes against
every rule of honesty; it would undercut our entire system of trade.
Jesus would never have condoned it! And yet, in one of his parables,
Jesus did speak of such a wicked servant as a wise man. Preposterous!

The reversal is also present in other Gospel stories. When a dispute
arises among his disciples, as to which of them is the greatest, Jesus
clearly states the upsidedownness of his kingdom in contrast to the
kingdoms of the world: "The kings of the Gentiles lord it over them;
and those in authority over them are called benefactors. But not so
with you; rather the greatest among you must become like the
youngest, and the leader like one who serves" (Luke 22:25–26). And
then Jesus goes on to present himself and his own position of service
as an example for his followers.

And perhaps most important for Latinos and Latinas who are often
dubbed "illegal," Jesus makes it very clear that those who are proud of
their strict obedience to the law will be surprised. They will find that
it is precisely to those whom the Pharisees and the strictly religious
people consider inferior, tainted, and disobedient to the law that Jesus
has come. It is with them that he repeatedly shares meals that are a
foretaste of the heavenly banquet.

A similar unexpected upsidedownness appears in Acts. Acts has
often been interpreted as a book of discipline, explaining how the first

church order appeared and tending to bolster the authority of the apostles and their successors. But a Latino reader of this book does not warrant such an interpretation. On the contrary, the book of Acts subverts the authority of the religious leaders of Israel, of the Roman Empire, and even of the church.

This is obvious at the very beginning of Acts, in the story of Pentecost. In that story, there are several subversive or upsidedowning notes. First, the text from Joel that Peter cites subverts all hierarchies based on age ("your young men" and "your old men") or gender ("your sons and your daughters," and "my slaves, both men and women"). This means that the traditional picture of Pentecost, where we imagine the Twelve with tongues of fire above their heads, is not true to the text, where those who receive the Spirit include men and women, young and old – literally "all flesh." But the story of Pentecost is subversive also in another way that Latinos find quite significant. Although all who speak are Galileans, those who receive their message do so in their own tongues. For Hispanics, living in a social atmosphere in which the "English-only" movement seems to gain ground, and in which they correctly understand that this is a xenophobic movement trying to marginalize them further, this is of prime importance. It is not we, nor even our open-minded English-speaking sisters and brothers, who reject such a movement, but the Holy Spirit of God. The first translator of the gospel is none other than the Holy Spirit. If there was an "Aramaic-only" movement in first-century Palestine – and we know that there were prejudices among the native Judeans against those other Diaspora Jews whom they called "Greeks" – the Holy Spirit pronounced a great and resounding "No!" And in Acts, as today, this is much more than a matter of language or culture. It says something very important about the "power of the Spirit" so often mentioned today. In Acts, the disciples receive the power of the Spirit, not to lord it over later converts or over their disciples, but so that those more recent disciples – Parthians, Medes, Elamites, etc. – may be fully part of the new community and will themselves have power to communicate the Gospel to others. If the Parthians can now proclaim the message in their own language, the first disciples will not be able to control or even understand what they are saying. Thus, what the Spirit has done is to empower the first disciples so that they may in turn empower others who will no longer be under their control. The power of the Spirit is not power for the disciples to keep, but rather power for the disciples to share. It is manifested, not so much in what authority one has, but particularly in how much authority others receive. In a church that has always had the tendency to become hierarchical and authoritarian, this is subversive indeed!

Many other examples from Acts could be adduced. There is no doubt that the problem of the Jewish leadership with the preaching of the early disciples is that their authority is being subverted. Indeed, through the first five chapters of Acts, "the people" are in favor of the new preaching, and it is the social and religious elite – the high priests, the elders, the Sadducees – that oppose the apostles and their preaching. Then, in ch. 6, when through a series of maneuvers the powerful are finally able to turn "the people" against the nascent Christian community, the Spirit subverts the very authority of the Twelve. They decide that they will retain the task of preaching for themselves, and that seven will be appointed to tend to administrative matters. But immediately after that decision, Stephen, one of the Seven, who is not supposed to be preaching, preaches the longest sermon in the entire book of Acts! In ch. 8, we turn to the ministry of another of the Seven. And in ch. 9, the story begins to focus on another who is neither one of the Twelve nor one of the Seven, but who is an outsider to the Christian community to the point of persecuting it. (Here again, we see another small example of how traditional interpretation has tended to whitewash those it considers its heroes. We hear much about Saul as a bystander, holding the clothes of those who stoned Stephen. But we do not notice that the case against Stephen had been concocted, among other, by people belonging to the synagogue of the Cilicians [Acts 6:9] and that this was most likely Saul's synagogue, for Tarsus was the capital city of Cilicia.) The authority of Paul himself is subverted in Acts, even after his conversion and during his mission. He has a vision of a Macedonian *man* – whose gender the text makes explicit. On the basis of that vision, he goes over to Macedonia, and what does he find? A group of women gathering for prayer. And out of that group of women emerges what was probably Paul's most faithful and supportive church.

THE PARABLE

The parable of the rich man and Lazarus has long played an important role in popular Latin American piety. San Lázaro is one of the most popular saints in Latin America, and also one of the most readily recognizable in Hispanic iconography. Throughout Latin America, and now also in the United States and Canada, there are Roman Catholic churches dedicated to San Lázaro. However, this is not the St. Lazarus that the church officially recognizes, the brother of Mary and Martha. This is the San Lázaro of the parable. As I write this essay, I have before me an image of San Lázaro, carved in wood and purchased in a mountain village in Peru. Typically, he is dressed in rags, carries a begging bowl, and is accompanied by a dog. Similar images may be found everywhere in Latin America and among Hispanics in the United States, not only in churches, but also in family altars. People flock to some of the churches devoted to San Lázaro, there to pray for healing, but particularly for their animals (San Lázaro always has at least one dog with him) and for economic salvation in times of dire need (San Lázaro is always dressed in rags and looks hungry).

After Vatican II, when there was a general purge in the list of saints who might be spurious, many priests and preachers tried to explain that this San Lázaro covered with rags and sores, and accompanied by dogs, is not the St. Lazarus that the church recognizes, but is rather a fictitious figure in one of the parables of Jesus. It was to no avail. People continued venerating the ragged San Lázaro, praying to him, and expecting miracles from him. The story is told of a church where a reforming priest substituted the real St. Lazarus for San Lázaro, placing a new image at the altar, and storing the old image in the sacristy, with the result that people ignored the official altar and were constantly finding excuses to go into the sacristy.

In more recent times – as the post-Vatican II reforming zeal has abated and new Roman Catholic theological currents have emerged – there is more interest in the actual religion of the people, and how this expresses both their real faith and Roman Catholic teaching. The result is that once again the fictional San Lázaro remains unchallenged by the official St. Lazarus, the brother of Mary and Martha.

Such popular devotion to San Lázaro is no accident. The reason behind it is that many believers feel that he is one of them – that he is as poor as they are, and therefore can understand their plight. Ornate baroque images of rich saints, decorated with gild, jewels, and crowns, deserve respect and admiration; but San Lázaro, with his sores and dogs, is more readily approachable, is more like us. It may even be that, precisely because churches were so richly decorated, because so many priests were distant from the flock – in some cases there being only one priest for every thirty-thousand believers – and because the Mass was said in a strange language, many among the poor felt closer to San Lázaro than to the church itself and its sacraments.

Significantly, although in English it is customary to refer to the parable in Luke as "the parable of the rich man and Lazarus," the traditional name in Spanish is "*la parábola de Lázaro y el hombre rico.*" Thus, interest is focused, at least at first, on Lazarus, and the rich man appears as part of the background for his story. As we shall see later, a closer examination of the text leads us to other conclusions. But at least the traditional Spanish name for the parable underscores a point that we often forget: The rich man has no name, but Lazarus does. This is one more of those "preposterous" touches in the parables of Jesus. The importance of a name in ancient times has been much discussed and need not detain us here. Suffice it to note that throughout Scripture – and in the Gospel of Luke itself, in the cases of John the Baptist and Jesus – the act of naming is significant. When Jesus gives the poor man a name, and lets the rich one remain nameless, he is already saying much about the relative worth of each. A name is important in practically every culture. Here we speak of "my good name," of "making a name for himself," and of "name recognition." The same is true – probably even more so – in Hispanic tradition, where the notion of honor is closely tied to the name. To confer a name on someone is to honor that person. Thus in 1711, when Bishop Gerónimo de Valdés (or Valdez) in colonial Havana decided to do something for the plight of abandoned children,[6] he not only founded a home for them but also decided that all the children in the home would bear the name of Valdés. Not to have a name is to be nobody. It is such a stigma that when one wishes to condemn a moral atrocity with the worst possible judgment, one says "*eso no tiene nombre*" – that has no name. Actually, one of the things that most Latino immigrants lose in coming to this country – and a loss that others find hard to understand – is part of their name. Traditionally, one carries at least two surnames: first the father's, then the mother's. Thus, the son of José Pérez and María Hernández would be Pedro Pérez Hernández. Traditionally, to have only one last name was a sign of illegitimacy. Even today, when illegitimacy is seldom a cause for discrimination, having a single last name does not speak well of one's mother. Furthermore, in official documents one often uses four last names, taking them alternatively from the father and the mother. Thus the son of José Pérez Prado and María Hernández Zapata would be Pedro Pérez Hernández Prado y Zapata. Upon entering the United States, this person becomes merely Pedro Pérez, which to him implies a breach with his extended family and its traditions.[7]

In this respect, the Latino experience in the United States brings significant elements into the picture. Before society at large, most

---

[6] Ondina E. González, "Consuming Interests: The Response to Abandoned Children in Colonial Havana," in *Raising an Empire: Children in Early Modern Iberia and Colonial Latin America* (ed. Ondina E. González and Pianca Premo; Albuquerque: University of New Mexico Press, 2007), 137–62.

[7] This way of naming people has its background in Spain. Apparently in traditional Amerindian cultures, and for quite some time among conquered Amerindians, surnames were not used. It was when they requested church services – particularly marriage – that many of them adopted surnames. Because at that point it was normally a priest telling them that they needed a surname, and suggesting one, many of the resulting names are religious in nature – names such as De la Cruz and Del Rosario. See Douglas Cope, *The Limits of Racial Domination: Plebeian Society in Colonial Mexico City, 1660–1720* (Madison: University of Wisconsin Press, 1994), 62–3.

Latinos – particularly recent immigrants and those without official documents – are nameless. They do landscaping and construction work. They harvest lettuce and grapes. They pump gas. They clean houses. Without them the entire economy of the nation will falter. Yet, they have no name. Most people who employ them do so indirectly, and never bother to learn their names. If they do, they only know that they are José or María, but do not know their last names, which in Hispanic culture is such a part of identity. The owner of the house has a name, often written in bronze by the mailbox. The one who cuts the grass has no name. In such a setting, we know who is "somebody" and who is "nobody."

In Jesus' preposterous story the poor man has a name, and the rich man does not. The rich man has a house, and a well-stocked table, and servants, but no name. Lazarus has nothing but rags, hunger, and dogs, but he has a name! And a name given by Jesus! Thus, to the Latino or Latina reader, whose name is ignored by those with a name – and who perhaps is even using a false name to avoid deportation – the story of San Lázaro is a vindicating story: Like Lázaro, I too have a name, and God knows it, even if the rich will not allow me to enter their homes!

As one then turns to the parable itself as it appears in Luke, the setting is interesting. At the beginning of ch. 15, where Jesus begins the series of parables of which this one is part, he is being criticized by the Pharisees and the scribes because he is welcoming "tax collectors and sinners." Thus, in various ways all the parables that follow relate to that accusation and respond to it. Then, in 16:14, we are told that the Pharisees "were lovers of money." So the audience as Luke describes it is twofold: On the one hand, there are the traditionally excluded, the tax collectors and sinners – often considered such because they lacked the wherewithal to fulfill all the requirements of the law as the "religious" people understood them. On the other hand there are the scribes and Pharisees – the latter being characterized as "lovers of money." (With reference to the scribes, it should be noted that the parable is also about the law, but this point will be discussed later.) Within this dual audience, they are all hearing not only what applies to themselves as rich Pharisees or poor sinners, but also what applies to the others. Thus, the Pharisees and scribes would hear Jesus giving a name to the poor man Lazarus and letting the rich man remain anonymous. And the sinners and tax collectors would also hear the story of the rich man going to Hades and even there hoping that Abraham would put Lazarus at his service.

This is probably another reason why this particular parable has traditionally been so important among the poor in Latino culture. In the typical Latino church, rich and poor sit and listen together. (In older times there were often special places reserved for the rich, but that practice has disappeared almost entirely.) The poor hear what Jesus is saying about the rich, and they also know that the rich are hearing what Jesus is saying about them. The hearing of the story itself is like a brief parenthesis of vindication, a space where Lázaro and his kind are exalted, as an announcement and foretaste of the future to come. Unfortunately, in most Protestant churches in the United States, this is no longer the case. Our churches are generally segregated on the basis of economic class, education, and social standing. Therefore, very seldom do the rich have to confront this parable in the presence of the poor, or do the poor have the opportunity to hear it while the rich are also present. In the case of Latino churches, this social segregation is often augmented by the barrier of language, so that the rich, even if they were present, would not hear what is being said to the poor, or vice versa.

At any rate, the setting of the parable, as provoked by the Pharisees' love of money, indicates that this is certainly one of the crucial themes of the parable, and that at this point most traditional interpretations are correct. This is so obvious that it requires little elaboration. And it is equally obvious that a Latino interpretation of the parable will focus on issues of wealth and poverty. The parable is a vindication of the nameless poor over the rich who have a name for themselves – but a name that apparently God ignores. It is a vindication of those who are not allowed beyond the gates of a house over those who live in the house and keep the gates closed. It is a vindication – as announced in the Beatitutes and Woes of Luke 6:20–26 – of the hungry over those who are filled. Significantly, Lazarus, the poor man for whom the gates of the mansion were closed, is now "carried away by the angels," whereas the rich man whose gates were closed simply dies and is buried.

But the parable has other dimensions that are equally important from a Hispanic perspective. The parable is also about what is legal and what is not, about how the law is known and obeyed. In v. 14, Luke has told us that the Pharisees were lovers of money. Then in vv. 15–18, there is what appears to be a digression about the law and how to obey it. At first sight, it would seem that this digression has nothing to do with the parable that follows, which reverts to the theme of money and the love of it. But this is not the case. The parable is not only about money or about wealth and poverty. It is also about the law, about how one recognizes it, and about how one obeys it. As one reads the entire story, the parable does not end with the rich man being tormented in Hades with flames and thirst, but with Abraham's words about "Moses and the prophets." This is not just an added touch at the end of the story. It is a significant part of the story itself and of the point it is making. The Pharisees and scribes claim to be particularly faithful in their study and application of the law. Those others whose presence they abhor – the tax collectors and sinners – are unclean because they do not obey the law as they should. To use a word often heard today in the news and in political campaigns, they are "illegal." The Pharisees and scribes are clean; they have obeyed the law. They are what today we would call "law-abiding citizens" whose pride in their own obedience to the law leads them to think of others as "illegal."

When one takes this into account, the parable is also about the difficulty that the rich man and his family have in hearing and obeying the law. At the end of the story, the rich man asks Abraham to send Lazarus back, so that his brothers might be saved. It has often been said that apparently the rich man has not learned his lesson, for he still believes that Lazarus is there to serve him. We tend to think that he is just stubborn. But the fact is that obedience and disobedience shape character. The rich man is who he is, and acts as he acts, because of who he has been and how he has acted. This is what medieval theologians called a *habitus*, and Latino lore refers to it in the oft-quoted lines: "*Árbol que crece torcido, jamás su tronco endereza, pues se hace naturaleza el vicio con que ha crecido*" – that is, a tree that grows twisted never becomes straight, for the vice that shaped it has become its nature. The disobedience of the rich man not only makes him guilty; it also makes him disobedient.

Abraham responds that the brothers "have Moses and the prophets; they should listen to them." The rich man insists that, if Lazarus were to come back from the dead, this would certainly lead them to a different sort of life. But surprisingly, Abraham tells the rich man that his brothers, who would not listen to Moses and the prophets, would still remain unconvinced "even if someone rises from the dead." The problem of the five brothers – like that of their already dead sibling – is not that they did not know. It is that they did not obey. Or rather, it is that because they did not wish to obey they found the way not to know.

We tend to think that if only we knew what is right we would do it. That would certainly be the case, we believe, if such knowledge were confirmed by a miracle. But in Luke-Acts there are repeated instances in which people respond to a miracle not with belief or with obedience but with further disobedience or with mockery. In Luke 6:11, after Jesus restores the withered hand of a man, the scribes and the Pharisees do not respond by asking, as we should expect, what this meant about how they should repent, or follow Jesus, or otherwise mend their ways. On the contrary, Luke tells us that "they were filled with fury and discussed with one another what they might do to Jesus." And at the beginning of Acts, even in the face of the miracle of Pentecost, there are still those who mock what they see and explain it away by claiming that those who do share in the miracle are drunk. It is not only unbelief that leads to disobedience, but also disobedience that leads to unbelief. The scribes and Pharisees do not believe because they do not wish to obey. The man's brothers do not obey and will not obey no matter how great a miracle they see. One is reminded of Bonhoeffer's dictum: "Only he who believes is obedient, and only he who is obedient believes," which he further explains: "If we are to believe, we must obey a concrete command."[8]

The parable of the rich man and Lazarus is often used to argue that there is an unbridgeable gap between heaven and hell – or between Hades and the bosom of Abraham – and that once one dies there is no crossing that gap. But in fact, the parable puts the gap much closer to us. The gap is not there only after death. The gap is already there in the present life. The rich man and his brothers, in closing their gates to Lazarus, are also closing the gates between their destiny and that of Lazarus. They are closing the gates because they do not wish to obey what is clearly the commandment of Moses and the prophets, to care for the poor and needy. The gap between the Pharisee and the sinner, between the rich and the poor, between the law-abiding and the illegal, exists already in the present order, in that the Pharisee, the rich, and the law-abiding refuse to see the sinner, the poor, and the illegal as their brother or sister.

Within its context, the parable thus seems to say that the strict adherence of the Pharisees and scribes to the minutiae of the law, thus claiming that all those other people who do not obey such precepts are unclean and unworthy sinners, is in fact a way in which they hide their grosser disobedience to the very heart of the law – the love of neighbor and of God. In today's vocabulary, they insist that they are "law-abiding citizens," and that these others are "illegal," because they wish to cling to their privilege and to the illusion that they are indeed more godly than "those others."

The parable then becomes even more ironic because when one reads it within the context of the entire Gospel of Luke, the one saying that "they will not be convinced even if someone rises from the dead" is Jesus, who will himself rise from the dead. In a way, Jesus is announcing that those who choose not to believe, because belief would require unwanted obedience, will continue disbelieving even after his resurrection. It may then be said, in passing, that the commonly held notion, that the main function of the resurrection is to prove that

[8] Dietrich Bonhoeffer, *The Cost of Discipleship* (New York: Macmillan, 1955), 56.

Jesus was indeed the Savior and the Son of God, is contradicted by the words of Jesus himself. In early Christian theology, the significance of the resurrection was not reduced to a grand miracle, of a final seal of approval on God's part – but that is a matter to be discussed elsewhere.

Like every parable, this one invites us – requires us – to find ourselves in the story. As we read, do we stand among the poor, next to Lazarus? Do we stand with the rich man, whose gates and table were closed to the poor? Do we stand with the five brothers, going along our merry way, with no regard for the poor or for the real spirit of the law, and perhaps offering as an excuse that we have not seen a miracle telling us what to do? Most probably, each one of us fits each of those various roles at different times and within the context of different relations. It is not only the law-abiding citizen whose ancestors migrated to the United States generations ago who discriminates against the illegal. It is also many earlier Hispanic immigrants who wish to make quite clear that they are different. In the latter case, it is such Hispanics who take the place of the rich man in the parable. This plurality of roles reflects the plurality of relationships in which Hispanics in the United States find themselves. Earlier, legally authorized immigrants are like the rich man when relating to the more recent immigrants, particularly those lacking documents; but they often are like Lazarus vis-à-vis the dominant culture. Among the more recent, undocumented immigrants, some have employment and some sort of documents, whereas others have no documents and must stand on a street corner waiting for an odd job. Poor Latino men are often looked askance by many in society, but have an unwarranted authority at home. All of this implies that we cannot – or should not – read the parable in a Manichean fashion, as if the world were divided between the rich and the poor, between oppressors and oppressed. The fabric of society is much more complex than that, and the parable invites and requires us to place ourselves at both ends of the equation.

The reference to the resurrection then leads us also to look at the parable christologically. The parables of Jesus are not just good, solid, moral teaching. They are also parables about the kingdom and about he who brings it in – Jesus himself. Where does Jesus fit in the parable?

Clearly, he is the one who comes from the dead, and in whom those who have reason not to obey will still not believe. But he is also the counterpart of the rich man. At this point, one is reminded of Paul's words to the effect that Jesus, who "though he was rich, yet for your sakes he became poor, so that by his poverty you might be enriched" (2 Cor 8:9). Thus in a way, Jesus himself, through his incarnation and his earthly life, is the alternative to the disobedient rich man in the parable. He did not remain aloof, but joined the poor for their sakes, so that they might be enriched. If we understand this phrase in Paul as somehow referring to having access to the kingdom, this dimension of the parable becomes even clearer. The rich man remained rich, and in so doing he closed the gates of his house to the poor, and closed the gates to the bosom of Abraham for himself. Jesus, being rich, became poor, and in so doing he opened to the poor the gates to the riches of the kingdom.

But the reference to the resurrection also makes the parable cut deeper. The rich man urges Abraham to send Lazarus back, so that his brothers may be warned, and Abraham tells him that they will not believe even if someone comes back from the dead and tells them. Now we stand in postresurrection times. What the rich man wanted for his brothers, and could not get, we have been given. One has indeed come back from the dead, and we have his words and his warnings. And yet we do not obey. Thus, we must consider a different option in placing ourselves in the parable. The choice is not just between the rich man and Lazarus. There is also the very likely possibility that we – the entire church – are most like the five brothers who remain behind, with the added liability that we have been told as they were not.

I said earlier that there is a disquieting, even subversive, tone to the Gospel of Luke. The parable of Lazarus and the rich man – and of the latter's five brothers – calls into question much of the manner in which we Christians have organized our lives, and particularly the manner in which the church has organized its life. The church, standing after the resurrection, has even less excuse than the five brothers for not heeding what the law and the prophets, and the Risen One, say and require regarding justice.

Suggestions for Further Reading

HISTORICAL CRITICISM

Barbour, R. S. *Traditio-Historical Criticism of the Gospels: Some Comments on Current Methods*, Studies in Creative Criticism 4 (London: SPCK, 1972). An important, though dated, introduction to the tradition criticism.

Bauckham, Richard. *Jesus and the Eyewitnesses: The Gospels as Eyewitness Testimony* (Grand Rapids, Mich.: Eerdmans, 2006). Challenges pessimistic views based on widely held understandings of oral transmission and standard form-critical perspectives regarding the historical veracity of the Gospels.

Bultmann, Rudolf. *History of the Synoptic Tradition* (New York: Harper & Row, 1963). Together with Dibelius (see below), a classic form-critical study.

Conzelmann, Hans. *The Theology of St. Luke* (London: Faber & Faber, 1960). The pioneering work on redaction criticism of the Gospel of Luke.

Dibelius, Martin. *From Tradition to Gospel* (New York: Charles Scribner's Sons, 1935). Together with Bultmann (see above), a classic form-critical study.

Meier, John P. *A Marginal Jew: Rethinking the Historical Jesus*, vol. 1, ABRL (New York: Doubleday, 1991). A useful restatement regarding the practice of tradition criticism, including a good discussion of the criteria of authenticity in the study of the historical Jesus.

Metzger, Bruce M. *The Text of the New Testament: Its Transmission, Corruption, and Restoration*, 3rd ed. (New York: Oxford University Press, 1992). A standard textbook on text criticism of the New Testament.

Neyrey, Jerome H., ed. *The Social World of Luke-Acts: Models for Interpretation* (Peabody, Mass.: Hendrickson, 1991). A useful collection of essays demonstrating the promise of social-scientific approaches to historical study of the Gospel of Luke.

Porter, Stanley E., ed. *Handbook of Classical Rhetoric in the Hellenistic Period, 330 B.C.–A.D. 400* (Leiden: Brill, 1997). A collection of primary sources concerned with the principles and practice of ancient rhetoric.

Rothschild, Clare K. *Luke-Acts and the Rhetoric of History: An Investigation of Early Christian Historiography*, WUNT 2:175 (Tübingen: Mohr Siebeck, 2004). An important investigation into the question of what it means to refer to Luke-Acts as "history."

FEMINIST CRITICISM

Anderson, Janice Capel. "Mapping Feminist Biblical Criticism: The American Scene, 1983–1990," *Critical Books in Religion* (ed. Eldon Jay Epp; Atlanta: Scholars Press, 1991), 21–44. Maps the development of American feminist criticism of the Bible in its early years.

Cheney, Emily. *She Can Read: Feminist Strategies for Biblical Narrative* (Valley Forge, Penn.: Trinity, 1996). Draws on feminist literary criticism and feminist biblical scholars to offer strategies for reading biblical texts in the service of feminist preaching.

Levine, Amy-Jill, with Marianne Blickenstaff, ed. *A Feminist Companion to Luke* (London: Sheffield Academic Press, 2002). Important collection of essays demonstrating a variety of ways feministic criticism has approached the Gospel of Luke.

Murphy, Cullen. *The Word According to Eve: Women and the Bible in Ancient Times and Our Own* (Boston: Houghton Mifflin, 1998). Written for a more general audience, this book surveys American feminist biblical criticism.

Reid, Barbara. *Choosing the Better Part? Women in the Gospel of Luke* (Collegeville, Minn.: Liturgical, 1996). After situating a feminist-liberationist hermeneutic in relation to other forms of biblical interpretation, this book examines the roles and portraits of women in the Gospel of Luke.

Schüssler Fiorenza, Elisabeth. *In Memory of Her: A Feminist Theological Reconstruction of Christian Origins* (New York: Crossroad, 1983). One of Schüssler Fiorenza's many contributions to feminist-critical study of the NT, this is now a critical classic.

Seim, Turid Karlsen. *The Double Message: Patterns of Gender in Luke-Acts* (Edinburgh: T. & T. Clark, 1994). A nuanced analysis of the roles of women in Luke-Acts.

NARRATIVE CRITICISM

Abbott, H. Porter. *The Cambridge Introduction to Narrative* (Cambridge: Cambridge University Press, 2002). An introductory survey of the state of the art in narratology.

Marguerat, Daniel, and Yvan Bourquin. *How to Read Bible Stories: An Introduction to Narrative Criticism* (London: SCM, 1999). A good alternative to Powell (see below), interacting more explicitly with literary and narrative work outside of biblical studies.

Merenlathi, Petri. *Poetics for the Gospels? Rethinking Narrative Criticism*, SNTW (London: T. & T. Clark, 2002). For persons already familiar with the landscape of narrative criticism, an engaging discussion of how the discipline is evolving (and might develop further).

Powell, Mark Allan. *What Is Narrative Criticism? GBS* (Minneapolis, Minn.: Fortress, 1990). The standard introduction to the field for NT students.

Rhoads, David, and Kari Syreeni, eds. *Characterization in the Gospels: Reconceiving Narrative Criticism.* JSNTS 184 (Sheffield: Sheffield Academic Press, 1999). For persons already familiar with the landscape of narrative criticism, an engaging discussion of how the discipline is evolving (and might develop further).

LATINO(A) CRITICISM

González, Justo. *Santa Biblia: The Bible through Hispanic Eyes* (Nashville, Tenn.: Abingdon, 1996). An essential entrée into reading the Bible through the lens of Latino(a) experiences.

Segovia, Fernando F. "Reading the Bible as Hispanic Americans," *New Interpreter's Bible*, vol. 1: *General and Old Testament Articles, Genesis, Exodus and Leviticus* (Leander Keck, ed.; Nashville, Tenn.: Abingdon, 1994), 167–73. A clear, brief introduction from one of the principal voices in Hispanic and intercultural interpretation.

Segovia, Fernando F., and Mary Ann Tolbert, eds. *Reading from This Place*, Vol. 1: *Social Location and Biblical Interpretation in the United States* (Minneapolis, Minn.: Fortress, 1995). Covers the terrain for understanding contextual readings from a range of social groups in the United States.

COMMENTARIES ON THE GOSPEL OF LUKE

These one-volume commentaries, reflecting a broad continuum of feminist commitments, provide introductory interpretive resources related to feminist criticism as well as feminist commentary on the Gospel of Luke: Elisabeth Schüssler Fiorenza, ed., *Searching the Scriptures: A Feminist Commentary* (New York: Crossroad, 1993); Carol A. Newsom and Sharon H. Ringe, eds., *Women's Bible Commentary*, 2nd ed. (Louisville, Ky: Westminster John Knox, 1998); and Catherine Clark Kroeger and Mary J. Evans, eds., *The IVP Women's Bible Commentary* (Downers Grove, Ill.: InterVarsity, 2002).

Bock, Darrell L. *Luke*, 2 vols., BECNT 3 (Grand Rapids, Mich.: Baker, 1994/96). Historical criticism.

Bovon, François. *Luke*, Hermeneia (Minneapolis, Minn.: Fortress, 2002). In progress, a multivolume study combining literary analysis, tradition criticism, and an interest in the history of interpretation.

Fitzmyer, Joseph A. *The Gospel according to Luke*, 2 vols., AB 28-28A (Garden City, NY: Doubleday, 1981/85. Redaction criticism.

Green, Joel B. *The Gospel of Luke*, NICNT (Grand Rapids, Mich.: Eerdmans, 1997). Narrative criticism and social-cultural criticism.

Johnson, Luke Timothy. *The Gospel of Luke*, SP 3 (Collegeville, Minn.: Liturgical, 1991). Literary criticism and historical background.

Marshall, I. Howard. *The Gospel of Luke: A Commentary on the Greek Text*, NIGTC (Grand Rapids, Mich.: Eerdmans, 1978). Redaction criticism.

Nolland, John. *Luke*, 3 vols., WBC 35 (Dallas: Word, 1989–93). Composition criticism.

Index of Scripture and Other Ancient Sources

Index of Modern Authors